The BEGINNER'S GUIDE to ELECTRIC GUITAR

GEAR, TECHNIQUE, AND TONS OF RIFFS

BURGESS SPEED

D1743407

Alfred, the leader in educational music publishing, and the National Guitar Workshop, one of America's finest guitar schools, have joined forces to bring you the best, most progressive educational tools possible. We hope you will enjoy this book and encourage you to look for other fine products from Alfred and the National Guitar Workshop.

This book was acquired, edited, and produced by Workshop Arts, Inc., the publishing arm of the National Guitar Workshop.

Nathaniel Gunod, acquisitions, managing editor
Burgess Speed, acquisitions, senior editor, music typesetter
Timothy Phelps, interior design
CD recorded by Collin Tilton at Bar None Studio, Northford, CT
Burgess Speed (guitar), Matthew Liston (bass), Pete Sweeney (drums).

Interior Photographs
By Larry Lytle; Timothy Phelps; and Stella Jurgen (17 Designs, Mississauga, Ontario, Canada), courtesy of Vivian Clement; guitars on page 7 courtesy of Gibson USA.

Cover Photographs
Guitar courtesy of Gibson USA.
Marshall courtesy of Marshall Amplification.

Alfred Music Publishing Co., Inc.
P.O. Box 10003
Van Nuys, CA 91410-0003
alfred.com

ISBN-10: 0-7390-6540-8 (Book & CD)
ISBN-13: 978-0-7390-6540-2 (Book & CD)

 Contents printed on 100% recycled paper.

CONTENTS

 A compact disc is included with this book. This disc can make learning with the book easier and more enjoyable. The symbol shown to the left appears next to every example that is on the CD. Use the CD to help ensure that you're capturing the feel of the examples and interpreting the rhythms correctly. The track number in the center of the symbol corresponds directly to the example you want to hear. Track 1 will help you tune your guitar to this CD.

ABOUT THE AUTHOR

Burgess Speed is the senior editor for National Guitar Workshop Publications. He is also an award-winning author, musician, performer, and educator. He graduated *summa cum laude* from Western Connecticut State University with a B. A. in music. Burgess has been playing guitar for over 30 years, and has performed and recorded in the genres of rock, blues, jazz, classical, folk, and just about every other kind of music you can imagine. Burgess lives in Connecticut with his wife Kimberly and their four children.

Acknowledgements

Thank you, Kimberly, for your love, support, and invaluable contributions to this project; and thank you for the beautiful dream that we are living together. Thank you, Jack, Spencer, Holden, and Delaney, for your inspiration and electricity. Thank you, Mom, for all of your support through the years, and all of those guitar lessons. Thank you, Uncle Dave, for introducing me to the guitar and being my first teacher. Thank you, Nat and Dave, for sticking with me when times were tough. Thank you, Tim and Donny, for your outstanding work on this book. Thank you, Gayle, John, Jake, and Ed, for proofing this book and for all of your suggestions. Thank you, Jason and Jim, for your input on the listening guide. Thank you, Stella and Vivian, for granting permission to use your photos. And thank you, Matthew, Pete, and Collin, for your great work on the CD.

Introduction

Welcome to the *The Beginner's Guide to Electric Guitar*. The whole point of this book is to get you up to speed as quickly as possible on:

1. The electric guitar and how it works

2. Gear and accessories (amplifiers, effects, strings, etc.) and how to use them

3. Electric guitar technique and how to play a lot of great riffs and songs

An electric guitar works by converting the vibrations of its strings into an electrical current, which is then amplified by a guitar "amplifier." The first electric guitar was made in 1931. This invention was desirable to jazz musicians who wanted to compete with the volume of louder instruments in their groups. (Nowadays, electric guitarists have no trouble blasting out drummers or other musicians in the band. In fact, we can be pretty obnoxious. But who can help it, with all of that power and volume at our disposal?) The creation of the electric guitar brought the instrument to the forefront of the stage. Jazz guitarists were now able to take solos, whereas before, they were relegated to the background of basic rhythm playing. The electric guitar also gave birth to the most electrifying musical genre of all time, rock 'n' roll. After that, the evolution of the guitar and electric guitar playing could not be stopped, as evidenced by the lineage of electric guitar greats. From Chuck Berry, Jimi Hendrix, and Jimmy Page, to Eddie Van Halen, Steve Vai, and Buckethead, guitar styles and technologies have continued to develop in new and astonishing ways.

The first two parts of this book (Gear, and Technique and Tuning) can be read straight through or just used as a reference. If you want to get right to playing songs and riffs, you can skip ahead to Part 3 (Playing Electric Guitar, page 18).

Although there are 7-, 8-, 9-, and even 12-string guitars, this book is concerned with the basic 6-string, electric guitar that we've come to know and love. Now, relax, open these pages, and start learning and playing. And remember, it's not hard to sound great and have a lot of fun.

PART 1: GEAR

PARTS OF THE GUITAR–ILLUSTRATION

Let's start by getting to know a little about the guitar's anatomy. Below is a picture of an electric guitar, a Fender Stratocaster to be precise. This is an extremely popular electric guitar. All of the parts are labeled, and to the right of this picture are some features found on other types of electric guitars. Page 5 provides brief explanations for all of the parts in the pictures below. The parts are numbered so you can easily locate the explanations on the next page.

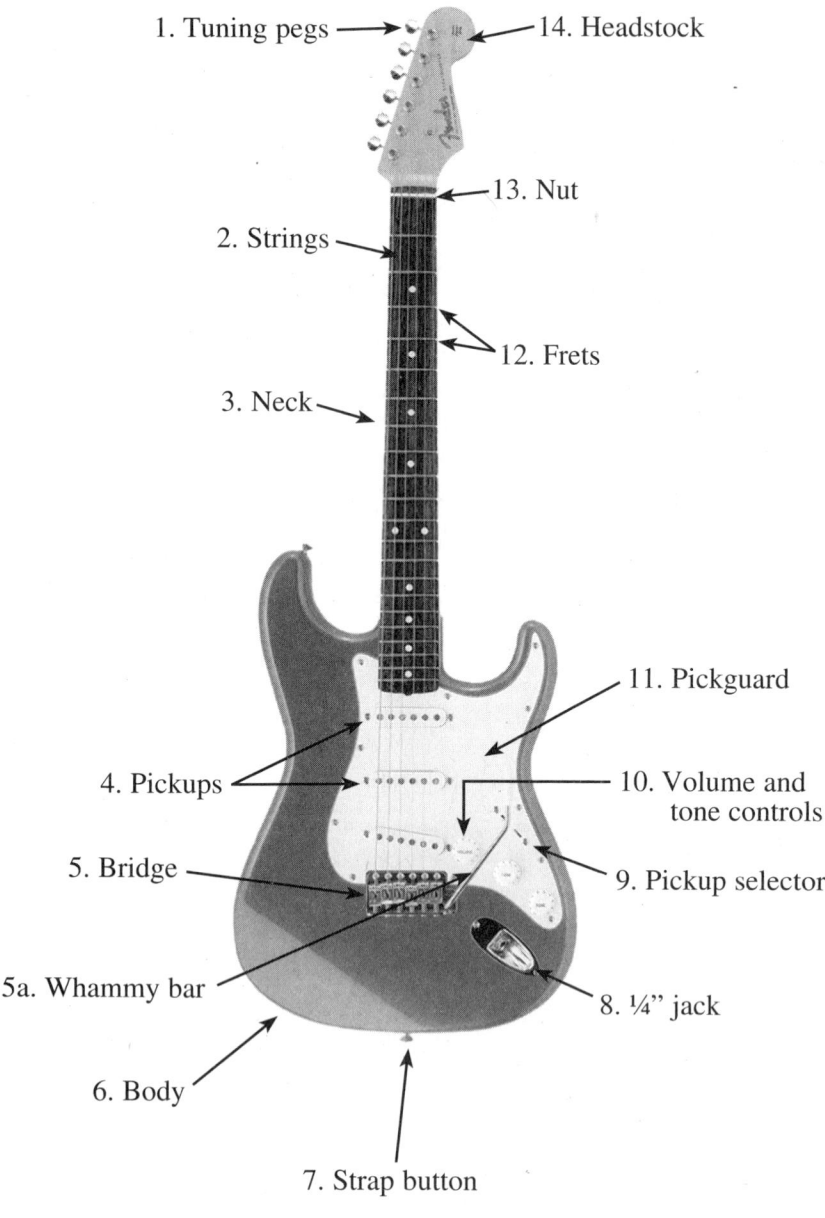

1. Tuning pegs
14. Headstock
13. Nut
2. Strings
12. Frets
3. Neck
11. Pickguard
4. Pickups
10. Volume and tone controls
9. Pickup selector
5. Bridge
5a. Whammy bar
8. ¼" jack
6. Body
7. Strap button

4b. Double-coil pickups (without covers).

4b. Double-coil pickups (with covers).

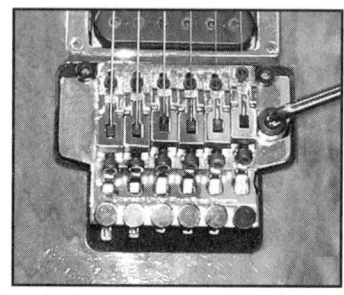

5b. Locking tremolo bridge.

5c. Non-tremolo bridge.

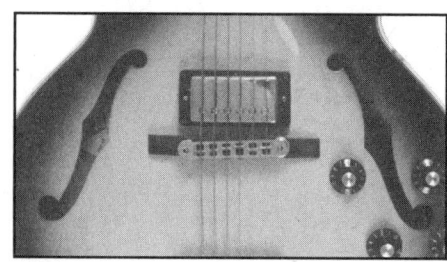

6a. F-holes.

PARTS OF THE GUITAR—EXPLAINED

1. Tuning pegs. These are used to tune your guitar by tightening or loosening tension on the strings. Tightening the string raises its *pitch,* and loosening the string lowers its pitch. ("Pitch" refers to the highness or lowness of a musical tone.)

2. Strings. Steel or nickel wires that are stretched across a guitar fretboard. These are what you pick and strum to make music. (For more on strings, see page 10.)

3. Neck. The long, skinny part of the guitar. The front part of the neck, on which the frets are embedded, is called the *fretboard.*

4. Pickups. These "pick up" the vibrations of the strings and convert them into an electrical current. There are two types of pickups:

> **4a. Single coil.** (As seen on the Stratocaster.) See page 6.

> **4b. Double coil.** See page 6.

5. Bridge. The bridge supports the strings and anchors them to the body. There are two types of bridges: *tremolo* and *non-tremolo.* A tremolo bridge has a whammy bar (see 5a in picture on page 4). By pushing or pulling the whammy bar, you can increase or decrease tension in the strings, thereby changing the pitch. With a whammy bar, you can drastically change the pitch with one quick move. On the Stratocaster, you see a non-locking tremolo bridge. Use of the whammy bar with this type of bridge can cause the guitar to go out of tune very easily. Because of this, the next type of tremolo bridge was developed.

> **5b. Locking tremolo bridge.** This type of tremolo bridge features clamps, which lock the strings in place to prevent them from going out of tune.

> **5c. Non-tremolo bridge.** A non-tremolo bridge supports the strings and anchors them to the body—it does not feature a whammy bar. This type of bridge is more apt to hold its tuning than a non-locking tremolo bridge, and some guitarists prefer the more resonant tone of these bridges due to their direct contact with the body.

6. Body. Usually made out of wood, this is the biggest part of the guitar, where the bridge, pickups, and tone controls are located. Some bodies are solid, some are hollow, and some are semi-hollow (see pages 6–7).

> **6a. F-holes.** Soundholes in the shape of an "f" located on either side of the bridge of many hollow-body and semi-hollow-body guitars.

7. Strap button. There are two of these on the guitar body, where the two ends of the strap are attached.

8. ¼" jack. You plug one end of your guitar cable here, and the other end into your amplifier.

9. Pickup selector. This appears as a lever or switch on most guitars. By selecting the pickup closest to the bridge, you get a thin, trebly tone. By selecting pickups closer to the fretboard, you get a thicker, bassier tone.

10. Volume and tone controls. You can fine tune the bass and treble frequencies on your guitar with the tone knobs, and of course, the loudness with the volume knob (or knobs). (See page 13 for more on bass and treble.)

11. Pickguard. This is a plastic plate under the strings that protects the body from being scratched or marked up by the guitar pick.

12. Frets. Metal wires embedded in the fretboard that delineate one note from another.

13. Nut. The nut is usually made out of plastic or stainless steel. It is located where the neck meets the headstock. The grooves in the nut guide the strings from the tuning pegs onto the fretboard.

14. Headstock. The headstock tops off the guitar neck. It supports the tuning pegs that control the tension and pitch of the strings.

CHOOSING AN ELECTRIC GUITAR

When choosing an electric guitar, there are two things to consider:

1. What sounds good to you
2. What feels good to you

You may like the sound of a particular guitar, but if it doesn't feel comfortable, you won't want to play it, and vice-versa. It is very important to visit a local music store and spend some time trying out the various types of guitars available to you. Remember, choose one that is comfortable and sounds good. There are two main types of electric guitars: *solid body* and *hollow body*.

Solid-Body Guitars

As its name implies, a solid-body electric guitar has a solid body, which contributes to its high level of *sustain* (the notes keep ringing without dying out). You can play these guitars at loud volumes, and you can use lots of effects. Because of this, the solid-body guitar is the type of guitar used most often in rock.

There are two main types of solid-body guitars: those with single-coil pickups and those with double-coil pickups. (There are also some that have a combination of both, but we'll limit our discussion to these two main types.)

Single-Coil Guitars

The single-coil guitar has a bright, twangy sound often associated with blues, funk, and country music. However, it is also widely used in different types of rock music. These guitars have a great sound, but they also come with challenges. The biggest issue is that single-coil pickups sometimes make a "humming" sound because they are susceptible to outside signal interference. (If you find the hum is too loud, make sure your guitar is facing away from your amplifier, and move further away from your amp, if necessary.)

*Fender Stratocaster
(single-coil pickup guitar).*

Examples of single-coil guitars are the Fender Telecaster and the Fender Stratocaster (see photo top right). The Stratocaster, or "Strat," is the quintessential single-coil guitar and has been used by Eric Clapton, Stevie Ray Vaughan, Jimi Hendrix, and countless others.

Double-Coil Guitars

Double-coil pickups consist of two single-coil pickups, positioned side-by-side, that are wired together in such a way that the "humming" created by single-coil pickups is cancelled, or "bucked." (Hence, their alternate name: "humbuckers.")

Because these guitars consist of two double-coil pickups, they are more powerful at lower volumes than single-coil guitars. They have a big, fat tone that works well with distortion (see page 14). Because of this, double-coil guitars are often associated with hard rock and heavy metal.

An example of this type of guitar is the Gibson Les Paul (see photo bottom right), used by Slash of Guns N' Roses, Jimmy Page of Led Zeppelin, Zakk Wylde of Black Label Society (and Ozzy Osbourne), and Neil Young. Another great example is the Gibson SG, used by Angus Young of AC/DC and Tony Iommi of Black Sabbath.

*Gibson Les Paul
(double-coil pickup guitar).*

Hollow-Body Guitars

The hollow-body electric guitar is completely hollow inside, with the exception of some wires. Because of its hollow body, this guitar has a deep, mellow, almost acoustic tone often associated with jazz, swing, and blues. The hollow body is not without its challenges, though—it causes feedback (so be careful of your volume!) and does not have the sustain of a solid-body guitar. Some hollow-bodies are equipped with single-coil pickups but most are made with humbuckers. Most hollow-body guitars can be identified by the f-holes; these are the soundholes in the shape of an "f" located on either side of the bridge. An example of a hollow-body guitar is the Gibson ES-175 (see photo below).

Semi-Hollow-Body Guitars

In addition to the standard hollow-body guitar, there is also the *semi-hollow-body guitar,* which was developed with a shallow body to help reduce feedback. Because a semi-hollow-body guitar has even less sustain than a standard one, many are made with a solid block of wood that runs through the center of the body. This increases sustain while also helping to minimize feedback. The quintessential semi-hollow-body guitar is the Gibson ES-335 (see photo below).

Even though hollow- and semi-hollow-body guitars are often used by jazz and blues players, many famous rock musicians have also made them their instruments of choice.

Players who have used hollow-body guitars are John Lennon, George Harrison, Eric Clapton, Steve Howe, Wes Montgomery, Grant Green, Pat Metheny, and Brian Setzer.

Gibson ES-175
(hollow-body guitar).

Gibson ES-335
(semi-hollow-body guitar).

GUITAR CASES AND WHAT TO KEEP INSIDE THEM

Okay, now that you've chosen your guitar, you'll need a case to protect it. There are two basic types of cases: a *hardshell* case and a *gig bag*.

Hardshell Case: A hardshell case offers the most protection. It consists of a solid covering, or "shell," often with a plush interior so that your guitar is snug and comfortable. These cases are fastened shut with buckles. Though hardshell cases offer the most protection for your guitar, sometimes they can be a little bulky. If you start to play out a lot, you may find them a bit cumbersome. (See photo top right.)

Gig Bag: A gig bag is a soft fabric covering, or bag, that more or less form-fits the guitar. You zip it open and closed, as opposed to the buckling and unbuckling of a hardshell case. Though gig bags do not offer as much protection for your guitar, they are extremely convenient. Because you can just strap them to your back like a backpack, they are easier to carry and actually allow you to carry more stuff (if you don't have a roadie). In addition to all this, you'll look like a pro and probably impress a lot of people. (See photo bottom right.)

The simple solution is to buy both a hardshell case for normal storage and a gig bag for when you're on the move.

Now, no matter what kind of guitar case you have, there is usually a pouch, pocket, or compartment inside where you can store some useful items. Following is a list of things you should keep in your case at all times.

- **Extra strings.** Strings wear out and occasionally break, so it's always good to have some extras on hand. You should have a full set, plus some individuals, especially the thinnest strings, as they break most commonly. (For more on strings, see page 10.)

- **Wirecutters.** Even though you could change your strings without these, they make the job much easier and quicker. (See photo below.)

- **String winder.** This is a cheap, useful tool for winding and unwinding strings. Like the pliers mentioned above, this also makes changing your strings quicker and easier. (See photo below.)

- **Picks.** Unless you intend to become a fingerstyle guitarist, it's always good to have extra picks. But keep your eye on those little buggers—they tend to grow legs and walk away, never to be seen or heard from again. (For more on picks, see page 11.)

- **Tuner.** Always keep one of these around. Whether you are playing by yourself, with your friends, or in front of thousands of people, your guitar needs to be in tune. (For more on tuners, see page 17.)

- **Cleaning cloth.** Wipe down your guitar with a microfiber cloth after every playing session. This helps get rid of dust, dirt, and oil residue from your fingers, which will, in turn, keep your guitar clean and minimize string rust.

- **Guitar cable.** Always keep an extra cable on hand. You never know when you or a friend will need one. (For more on guitar cables, see page 9.)

Hardshell case.

Gig bag.

Wirecutters.

String winder.

ACCESSORIES

Let's take a closer look at some accessories you'll need to begin playing electric guitar.

Cables

Aside from your guitar and amplifier, this is the next most important item. The cable, with a ¼" plug on each end, is what connects the guitar to the amplifier. Cables come in all lengths, from 6 inches to 50 feet. Even though they might be a little more expensive, high-quality cables will last a lot longer than inexpensive ones. There are straight cables and curly cables. Aficionados contend that different cables produce different guitar sounds. For this reason, and because they are easier to manage, most guitarists today use straight cables.

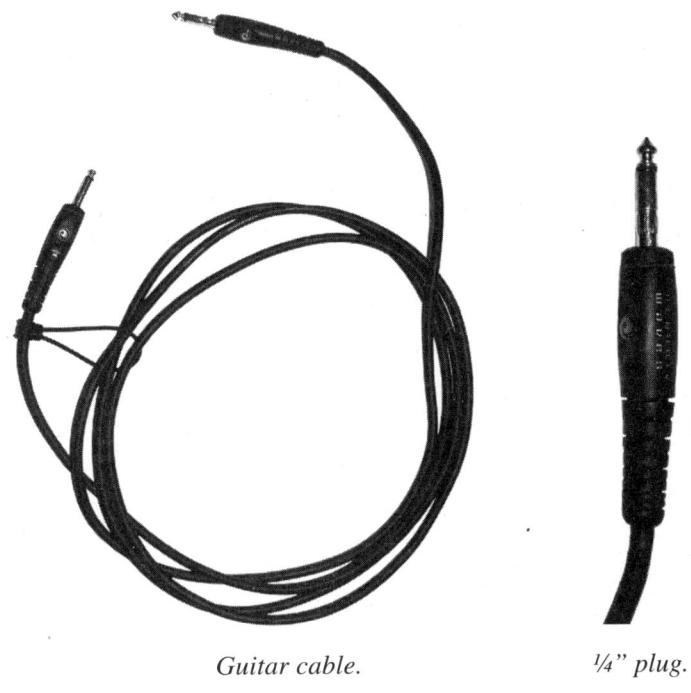

Guitar cable.   *¼" plug.*

Straps

In most cases, a guitar strap is fastened at the tail-end of the body and where the body meets the neck. There are many types of amusing straps you can purchase, like ones with skulls with fiery eyes on them, or ones with aliens, and so forth. However, as long as it is adjustable, attaches at both ends, and holds your guitar up, it's probably good enough. Wide leather straps are perhaps the most comfortable. Keep in mind that straps do not only have to be used while standing. Some prefer to use a strap even when sitting because it allows you to keep the guitar in the same position whether sitting *or* standing.

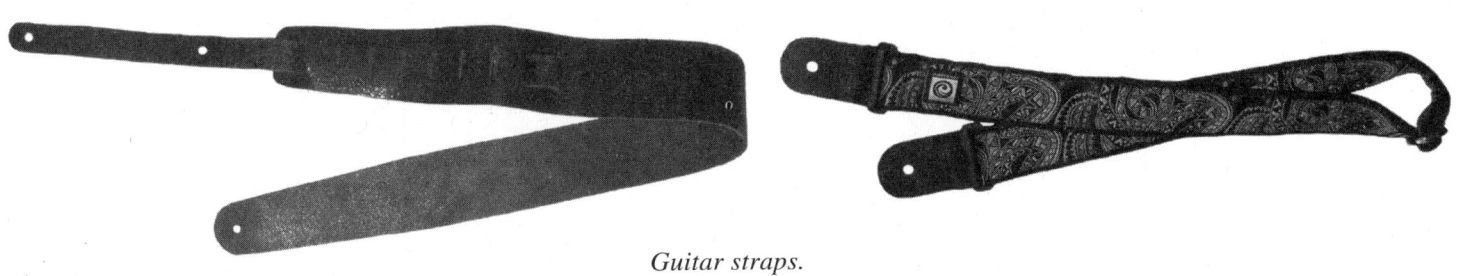

Guitar straps.

Strings

There are several factors to take into consideration when choosing guitar strings: *alloy* (the type of metal they are made of), *gauge* (string diameter), and *winding* (the finish on the surface of the strings).

Alloy: Electric guitar strings are either *stainless steel, nickel-plated,* or *pure nickel.* Stainless-steel strings are chosen for their brilliance of tone and durability. Their rough surface may, however, produce a bit of finger noise, or "squeaking." Nickel-plated strings are stainless-steel strings with a surface that is plated with nickel. You may lose some of the brilliance with these strings, but you also get rid of that pesky finger noise and gain a smooth surface conducive to fast lead playing. Finally, pure nickel strings are easy on the fingers and offer a mellow tone preferred by many jazz players.

Winding: Strings are either *round wound* or *flat wound.* The round-wound string consists of a wire that is wrapped around the string's core. This surface offers the loudest and most brilliant tone, but also significant finger noise. Flat-wound strings are wrapped in such a way as to create a smooth finish. Though finger noise is eliminated, so is the brightness of tone, which, again, is desirable to many jazz guitarists.

Gauge: The gauge of a string is measured in thousandths of an inch (an "8-gauge" string is 8 thousandths of an inch, or .008 inches). Sets of strings are usually referred to by the gauge of the thinnest string. Though manufacturers vary in their classifications, you can use the following as a guide (the gauge of the thinnest string is also indicated): extra super light (.008), super light (.009), regular light (.010), medium (.011), heavy (.012), and extra heavy (.013). Let's look at some generalizations that can be made about the thickness of your strings:

Lighter Strings

- The lighter the strings, the easier they are to play. Lighter gauge strings are easier to press against the fretboard. They are also easier for techniques such as bending and sliding.

- Lighter strings are more apt to break. In a set of 8- or 9-gauge strings, you may find that the high-E string breaks more often than you would like.

- Lighter strings have a thinner, more jangly sound.

Thicker Strings

- Thicker strings take more force to press against the fretboard.

- They have a fuller, "fatter" sound.

- Thicker strings break less often.

10-gauge strings are great to start with—not too light, not too heavy. All types of music can be played with this gauge, and you get a thick tone without chewing up your fingers.

Changing Your Strings

Strings have a bad habit of either wearing out or breaking. When either of these occurs, it's time to change them. At first, you can bring your guitar to a local music store and have them slap a new set on for a nominal fee. But after a while, this will prove inconvenient (especially when just replacing a single string). There is nothing to be intimidated about; with just a little practice, you'll be changing strings like a pro in no time. The following will take you step-by-step through the process.

If you have a locking tremolo bridge, start with the first step. If you have a non-locking tremolo bridge or a non-tremolo bridge, start with the third step.

Taking off the Old Strings

1. If your guitar has a locking nut, release it. (See Fig. 1.)
2. Insert a "spacer" (a piece of wood or cork) under the tail-end of the bridge to stop it from "floating." (See Fig. 2.)
3. With a string winder (or your fingers), loosen the tension on the strings by turning the tuning peg in a clockwise direction. Now, release the string lock (if you happen to have one) on your bridge saddle. (See Fig. 3.)
4. Clip the strings with wirecutters and remove them.

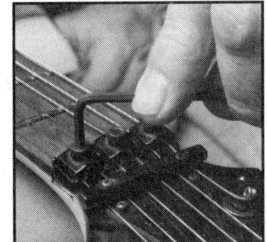
Fig. 1.

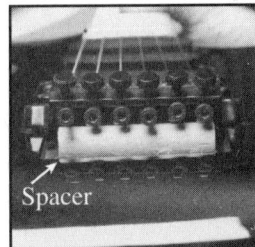
Spacer
Fig. 2.

Putting on the New Strings

1. Thread the new string through the appropriate hole in the bridge (on some guitars, like the Strat, you will have to send the string through the back of the body). Now, pull the string across the fretboard to the headstock.
2. Guide the string through the hole in the *capstan* (the post to which the string is attached). Pull the string up from the fretboard to ensure you can wrap it enough times around the capstan (see Fig. 4). This step takes a little practice; the thicker strings will need only two or three wraps, but as the strings become thinner, they will need more and more wraps to stay secure.
3. Now, crink the end of the string, using both hands to pull it in the same direction on either side of the capstan (see Fig. 5). This will help keep the string in place when performing the next step.
4. While maintaining pressure on the string with one hand, use the winder to tighten it, making sure that the string is wrapping around the capstan in a downward motion toward the headstock. As tension on the string increases, make sure it is snug in the correct saddle groove on the bridge as well as the correct groove in the nut. Clip off the excess string with wirecutters (see Fig. 6).
5. Repeat steps 1–4 for the remainder of the strings.

Fig. 3.

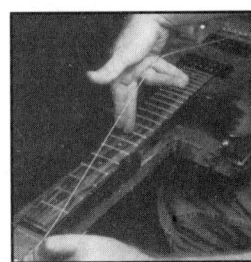
Fig. 4.

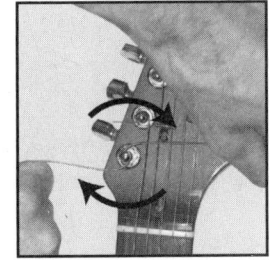
Fig. 5.

Fig. 6.

After changing the strings, stretch them out a bit by gently pulling them away from the fretboard (see Fig. 7). You may have to tune, stretch, and retune several times before the strings hold their tuning.

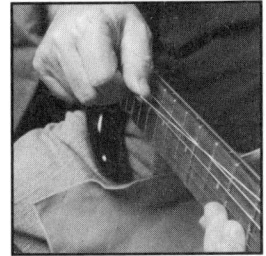
Fig. 7.

Picks

A pick looks like this:

Actual size

Picks come in a variety of shapes, sizes, and thicknesses. Some are made of plastic, some are made of metal, you may even find some made of strange, alien substances.

For most electric guitar playing, it is recommended that you use a regular thick plastic pick, as seen in the picture above. In time, feel free to experiment with other types and thicknesses.

For the curious:

- Thin picks are great for strumming and have a tinny, percussive tone. (They also get chewed up pretty quickly.)
- Thick picks produce a fatter, mellower tone and are great for lead playing. (They last a whole lot longer, too.)
- Medium picks are somewhere in between; they provide a good strumming tone, they're great for lead work, and they last longer than a thin pick.

AMPS

All right, now you have your guitar and a bunch of accessories. None of this will matter if you can't plug into an *amplifier*. An amplifier, or *amp,* takes the signal from an electric guitar and makes it louder. The tone of your guitar can also be altered by various controls (usually dials) on the amplifier. Some amps even come with effects such as *distortion, chorus,* and *reverb* (see page 14). If you are an absolute beginner, you will most likely only need a small practice amp at first. There are many small, inexpensive amps that will get you going in the right direction (anywhere from 5 to 30 watts will suffice). There are two main types of amplifiers: *tube* and *solid state.*

Tube Amps

The active electronic components in a tube amp are vacuum tubes. Tube amps have advantages and disadvantages. They are known for their deep, warm tone, as well as their propensity for natural *overdrive,* or distortion. Once a tube amp gets warmed up, there's nothing like it. The downside to tube amps is that they are heavy, require regular maintenance, and are very fragile—the glass vacuum tubes can be easily damaged when bumped around during transport or if they are exposed to extreme temperatures. Fender and Marshall are just two companies that make great tube amps. These amps are used in many types of music, but you will especially find the bright, clean sound of Fender in a lot of classic rock, blues, and country, and the gritty, warm distortion of Marshall in a lot of hard rock and heavy metal.

Back of a tube amp.

Solid-State Amps

The solid-state amp is powered by transistors instead of tubes. It is less expensive to produce, so in turn is less expensive to purchase. It is also less bulky, less heavy, and more durable (you can bang it around with less chance of damaging it). What's the downside here? It does not have the warmth and depth of tone of a tube amp. However, for some players, this "cold," bright tone is preferable. Jazz players often prefer solid-state amps for this reason. In recent years, great strides have been made in improving the sound of solid-state amps. In fact, there are even solid-state *modeling amps* that use digital technology to simulate the sounds of vintage tube amps.

Solid-state Line 6 modeling amplifier.

Amp Configurations

There are two main types of amp configurations: *combo* and *amp head and cabinet.* The combo amp is a single unit made up of the *preamp* (consisting of volume and tone controls as well as effects), *power amp* (which boosts the signal from the guitar and preamp), and the *speaker* or speakers (which broadcast the final sound). The combo configuration is the easiest to transport because it exists as one manageable unit. The amp head and cabinet setup is more bulky because it has a separate head (comprised of the preamp and power amp) and a separate cabinet housing the speakers. This configuration allows you to pair different heads and cabinets to achieve the sound you are looking for. Usually appearing as an amp head resting on top of a cabinet, this type of setup is known as a *half stack.* A *full stack* consists of an amp head resting on top of two speaker cabinets. Hence, the mythic "Marshall stack," legendary in the realm of heavy-metal folklore.

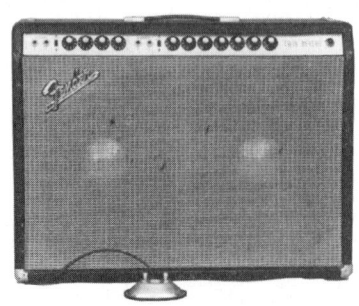

Combo amp.

Amp head and cabinet (Marshall half stack).

PLUGGING IN AND GETTING YOUR SOUND

Okay. Got your guitar? Got your amp? Let's plug in.

1. Plug your ¼" cable into the ¼" jack on your guitar.

2. Making sure that the power on your amplifier is off, plug the other end of the cable into the amp where it says "input."

3. Turn the volume all the way down on your guitar and amp just to ensure you don't accidentally blow out your ear drums when you plug in.

4. Turn the power on your amp "on" (usually indicated with a light of some sort).

5. Turn up the volume on your amp and guitar.

Now, it's time to work on your sound. Many amplifiers have at least three *EQ* (equalization) knobs: *bass, middle* (or *mid*), and *treble.* You will notice they all go from 0–10.

Amplifier EQ.

Bass is the low end, or low frequency, of your sound—the body and depth. Middle, or "mid-range," is just that—the middle frequencies where most guitar sounds naturally occur. Treble is the high end, or high frequency, of your sound. Below are some steps to follow when attempting to get your sound.

1. *Turn all three EQ knobs to their middle position, usually straight up at "5," or the 12 o'clock position.* Many amplifiers will sound good set up just like this. Now it becomes a matter of personal preference.

2. *Experiment with your bass knob.* Turn it up, and you will feel the rumble of your tone; go too far, and it will become muddy. Turn it down, and you may feel like the bottom fell out. Usually a position just to the right of middle is satisfactory.

3. *Play with your mid-range.* Most often, just to the right of the middle position is a satisfactory setting for this as well. Many heavy metal players will "scoop" their mids, which means to turn them way down. This produces an interesting, hollow, cave-like sound that you may like to experiment with.

4. *Play with your treble.* This is your attack and brightness. If you turn this way up, you will hear every little pick noise and scrape. Treble can really give an edge and bite to your sound. You may also have a *presence* knob. This controls frequencies even higher than treble. Often, the middle position is good for this control as well, but don't take my word for it: Experiment!

Keep in mind that you have volume, tone controls, and a pickup selector on your guitar (see pages 4–5). Both your guitar and amplifier work together to create your sound. Experiment with all of the controls.

Note: Your amplifier may also feature effects such as distortion (which would be controlled by the *gain* knob) and reverb. These effects, and others, will be discussed in the next section.

EFFECTS

Now that you have your fundamental sound, it's time to add some effects. Effects change, or alter, your sound and are available in two basic forms: *pedals* (also known as *stomp boxes*) and *digital multi-effects units.* A pedal consists of one effect per unit, while multi-effects units store many different effects. Although digital multi-effects units offer considerable variety, many guitarists prefer the vintage sound of basic stomp boxes. Stomp boxes can be placed in a *pedalboard,* which allows you to mix and match individual pedals to your liking. Following are some common effects you may find in an amp, pedal, or multi-effects unit. Be sure to check out the CD to hear how they sound.

2 **Distortion.** Distortion is also known as overdrive. It is the sound of overdriven vacuum tubes that fills the aural landscape of hard rock. When first simulated in a foot pedal, it was known as "fuzztone." There are many varieties of distortion, ranging from a slightly distorted, chunky blues tone to the warm, velvety, rich, and luxurious bath of sound found in classic heavy metal.

3 **Reverb.** This simulates the echo in a room after a fundamental sound is heard. Reverb can be adjusted to sound like you are playing in a small club or vast auditorium.

4 **Wah-wah pedal.** This foot pedal creates a sound often heard in funk, disco, and rock. By depressing and releasing the foot pedal, the tone is sent through a "funnel" of high and low frequencies, creating an effect that sounds much like its name: "wah-wah."

5 **Chorus.** This effect is produced by *sampling* (making a digital copy of) your original guitar sound, then slightly delaying and altering its pitch, and mixing it back together with the original. The result is a lush effect that sounds as if more than one guitar is being played.

6 **Delay.** This box samples your original sounds and plays them back. You can control the speed, volume, and duration of the sampled repetitions.

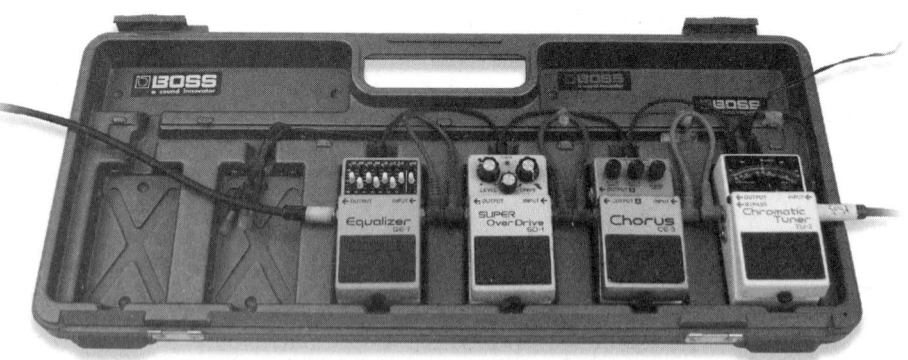

Pedalboards can be used to mix and match individual effects pedals.

Digital multi-effects units can store many effects in a small, convenient module.

PART 2: TECHNIQUE AND TUNING

Now you know enough about your gear to pick up your guitar and get ready to play. In Part 2, we'll be looking at the best ways to hold the guitar, the correct technique for your right and left hands, the six strings of the guitar, and how to tune.

Note: This book is written from a right-handed perspective (right hand is the picking/strumming hand and left hand is the fretting hand). If you are left-handed, you may reverse the instructions regarding right- and left-hand technique in this book.

HOLDING THE GUITAR

You can play guitar either sitting down (which you will probably do when practicing) or standing up (which you will most likely do when performing with others or for an audience).

Sitting

When playing guitar sitting down:

- Sit up straight!
- Rest the curve of the guitar body on your right leg.
- Tilt the neck of the guitar slightly upward.
- You should be able to easily reach any area of the fretboard with your left hand, and you should have no trouble reaching around the guitar with your right arm to pick or strum any of the strings.
- It is important to be comfortable when playing, but not so much so that you are in danger of falling asleep. Using a nice straight-back chair will help you achieve a balance between being comfortable and staying awake.

Note: You can use a strap even while sitting to help keep your guitar in the correct position.

Correct sitting position.

Standing

When playing guitar standing up:

- Stand up straight!
- Unless you feel like tiring your arms out quickly and looking silly, use a strap.
- Adjust the strap so that your guitar is positioned similarly to when you are sitting down. Obviously, you don't want to look too uncool by having the guitar positioned too high, but you also don't want it to be too low (even if some of your favorite rock stars disagree). Find the right height so that the guitar doesn't feel totally different when sitting or standing.
- Your left hand should have easy access to any location on the fretboard, and your right arm should comfortably reach around the body to access any of the strings.

Correct standing position.

LEFT- AND RIGHT-HAND TECHNIQUE

Your right hand is used to pick or strum the strings, while your left hand is used to "fret" notes (which means to press the strings against the fretboard to produce specific pitches). We will now look at the correct way to use your hands when playing guitar.

Right-Hand Technique

Holding the Pick

- Grip the pick between your thumb and index finger.

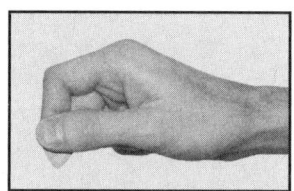

Holding the pick.

Position and Technique

- Place the heel of your hand on the bridge of the guitar, being careful not to block the strings (see right). This provides a pivot point and frame of reference for your hand, which makes it easy to play any string even when you're not looking. When strumming chords, you may remove the heel of your hand from the bridge and let it float freely. However, in this book, we will not be doing much chord strumming—*that's for acoustic guitarists!*

- Pluck the strings with the tip (pointy part) of the pick.

- When playing each string, try to use as little movement as possible; don't move your whole arm if all you need to do is slightly move your wrist and fingers. (Be lazy, don't expend more energy than you need to!)

Note: In this book, unless otherwise indicated, you will be using *downstrokes* of the pick (striking the string in a motion toward the floor).

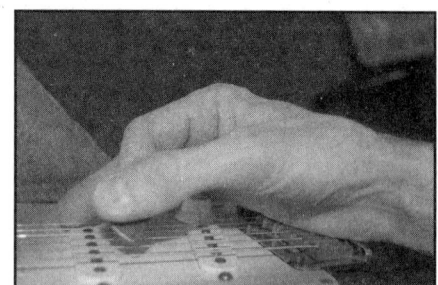

Correct right-hand position.

Left-Hand Technique

The fingers of the left hand are numbered 1–4 starting with the index finger (see right). These numbers will become important when you start reading TAB on page 18.

Thumb Position

Your left-hand thumb should be positioned at the back of the guitar neck, somewhere around the middle, and lined up with your index finger. If your thumb drifts up or down a bit, don't sweat it. Sometimes, it's okay to even hook your thumb over the top of the neck; guitar legend Jimi Hendrix did this all the time.

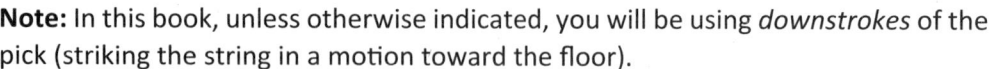

Left-hand fingers.

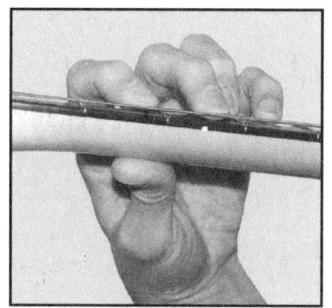

Correct thumb position.

Fretting Notes

You fret a note by pressing a string with a left-hand finger against the fretboard at a particular location (1st fret, 2nd fret, 3rd fret, etc.).

When fretting notes, it's important to:

- Curl your fingers.

- Always press the strings with your fingertips, not the pads, or flat parts of your fingers (unless you are using the "barring" technique, covered on page 44).

- Press the string just before, or to the left of, each fretwire. But remember, if you are too far left, it will be harder to press and will probably result in a buzzing noise when you pick the note.

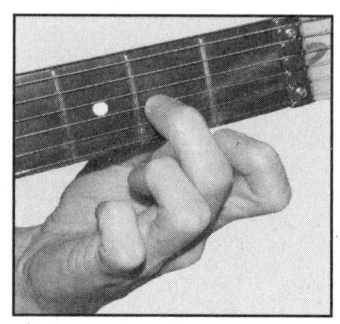

Correct way to fret notes.

THE SIX STRINGS AND TUNING YOUR GUITAR

The standard electric guitar has six strings.

- The fattest string—the one closest to the ceiling when you are playing the guitar—is the 6th, or low-E, string. Even though it is physically above the other strings, we call this the "bottom" string.

- The next string is the 5th, or A, string.

- Next is the 4th, or D, string.

- Then comes the 3rd, or G, string.

- That is followed by the 2nd, or B, string.

- Finally, we have the 1st, or high-E, string. This is also known as the "top" string.

These strings are anchored at the bridge, then cross over the fretboard and nut, and attach to tuning pegs that you either tighten or loosen to *tune* your guitar.

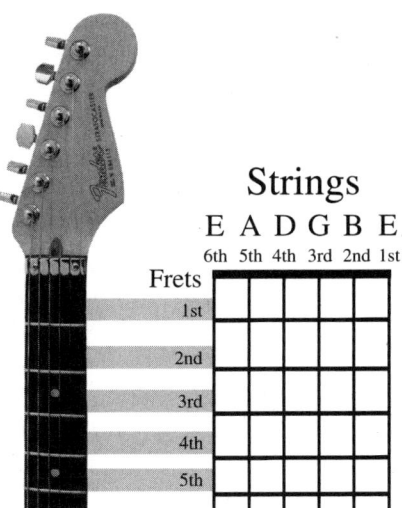

Tuning Your Guitar

The first thing you have to do before playing your guitar is make sure it is in tune. The strings have to be tuned to certain pitches in order for the guitar to sound good when you play. Stringed instruments do not stay in tune for long. Strings may slip, loosen, expand, or contract when the air is dry or humid, or when the temperature is hot or cold. As a general rule, you should check your tuning and make any necessary adjustments every time you play. There are several methods you can use to tune your guitar. We'll look at a few of these.

Electronic Tuners: Plug your guitar into an electronic tuner, play a note, and it will tell you either with a needle or an LED display if you are too low, too high, or on pitch. Play each string, then tighten or loosen the pegs until the tuner indicates the pitch is correct. This is a great way for beginners to tune. Not only will it help you get in tune quicker, but it will help develop your *musical ear* (the ability to discern the highness, lowness, or "sameness" of different pitches).

Electronic tuner.

Use the CD: If you already have a decent musical ear, you can try tuning to Track 1 of the CD included with this book. First, you will hear the 1st (high-E) string played several times. Play your open 1st string several times and try to tell if it is higher or lower than the pitch on the CD. If it is lower, turn the tuning peg counterclockwise to raise the pitch until it sounds correct. If it is higher, turn the tuning peg clockwise to lower the pitch until it sounds correct. Repeat this process with the remainder of the strings.

Relative Tuning: This method is the most challenging, but if you master it, you won't have to rely on a CD, an electronic device, or anything else to get yourself in tune. This is called "relative" tuning because the strings are tuned relative to each other. Here's how you do it:

1. Tune your 6th (low-E) string to a correct E pitch by using either a keyboard, another guitar, an online tuner, or some other device such as a pitch pipe. (On a keyboard, this pitch is found 12 white keys below middle C.) If you do not have any of these, just approximate the note as best as you can.

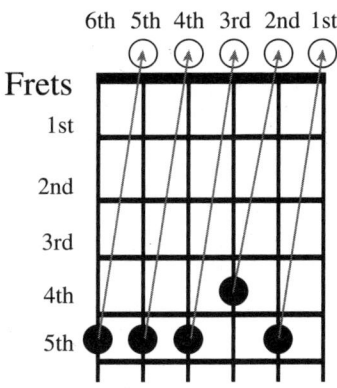

2. Play the 5th fret of the 6th string, then play the 5th string open. These pitches should match. If the 5th string sounds too low, raise the pitch. If it sounds too high, lower the pitch.

3. Play the 5th fret of the 5th string, then play the open 4th string. Match the pitches by adjusting your 4th string if necessary.

4. Play the 5th fret of the 4th string, then play the open 3rd string. Match the pitches by adjusting your 3rd string if necessary.

5. We momentarily go out of position for this one. Play the 4th fret of the 3rd string, then play the open 2nd string. Match the pitches by adjusting your 2nd string if necessary.

6. Finally, play the 5th fret of the 2nd string, then play the open 1st string. Match the pitches by adjusting your 1st string if necessary. You should now be in tune.

PART 3: PLAYING ELECTRIC GUITAR

LESSON 1: MUSIC NOTATION

Now we get to the fun part—playing the electric guitar. In this section, you'll learn all kinds of cool riffs, licks, and songs in the styles of groups like Metallica, Led Zeppelin, Pink Floyd, Black Sabbath, Rage Against the Machine, Nirvana, and more. But before we get to that, we have to learn some basics of music notation.

Reading Tablature (TAB)

In this book, we'll be using *tablature*, or *TAB*, to show how a piece of music is supposed to be played. Tablature is easy to learn. The TAB *staff* is made up of six lines, with each line representing a guitar string. The top line represents the 1st string (high E), the thinnest string. The line under that represents the 2nd string (B). The 3rd line represents the 3rd string (G). The 4th line represents the 4th string (D). The 5th line represents the 5th string (A). The bottom line represents the 6th string (low E), the fattest string.

TAB Staff

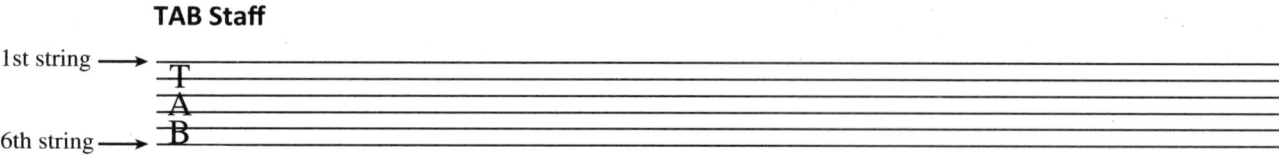

The numbers on the lines tell you what frets to play on what strings. For example, a "3" on the top line tells you to play the 3rd fret of the 1st string. Numbers underneath the TAB staff indicate which left-hand fingers to use. Remember (page 16), the fingers of the left hand are numbered 1–4, starting with the index finger. Check out the TAB examples below. Underneath the examples is an explanation of how to play each one (A, B, C, D, and E).

TAB Examples

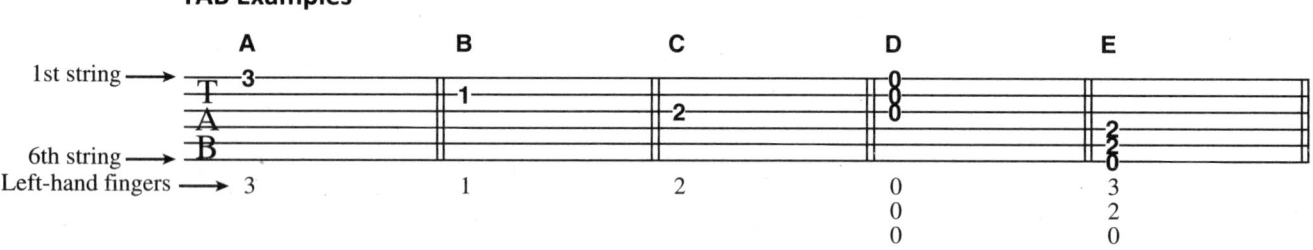

A = Play the 1st string at the 3rd fret using the 3rd finger

B = Play the 2nd string at the 1st fret using the 1st finger

C = Play the 3rd string at the 2nd fret using the 2nd finger

D = Play the open 1st, 2nd, and 3rd strings at the same time

E = Play the open 6th string
    Play the 5th string at the 2nd fret using the 2nd finger
    Play the 4th string at the 2nd fret using the 3rd finger
    all at the same time

Beats, Measures, Barlines, and Time Signatures

Rhythm is the organization of music in time. It's the part of a song that you can tap out with your hands on a table or your steering wheel while you're stuck in traffic. There are many components that contribute to rhythm, the first we'll look at are *beats, measures, barlines,* and *time signatures.*

- The **beat** is the pulse, or heartbeat, of the music.

- **Measures** divide music into equal sections, all containing the same number of beats.

- **Barlines** show where one measure ends and another begins. *Double barlines* indicate the end of a section or short example, while *final barlines* indicate the end of a song.

- The **time signature** appears at the beginning of a piece of music. It consists of one number stacked on top of another number. The top number tells you how many beats are in each measure, and the bottom number tells you what kind of note gets one beat. Most of the music in this book is in $\frac{4}{4}$, which means there are four beats in each measure and the quarter note (see below) gets one beat.

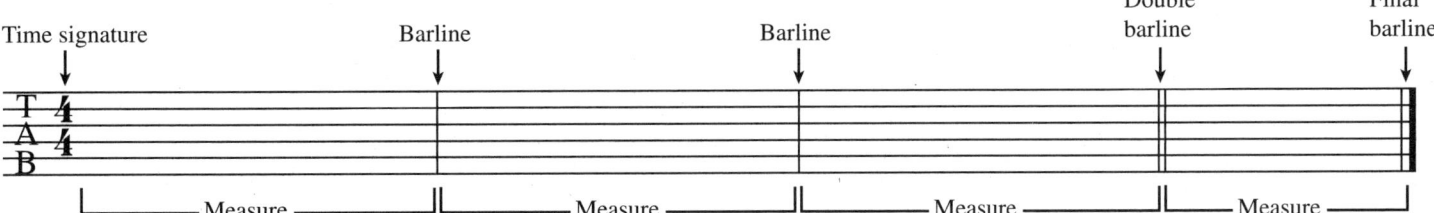

Notes and Rests

Notes and *rests* are also important aspects of rhythm. A note is a tone, or pitch, that lasts for a certain amount of time. In TAB, the numbers on the lines indicate notes. In this book, these numbers will also indicate a note *value,* or *duration,* for which the notes are supposed to last. This is done through the use of *circles, stems, beams,* and *flags.* When a number appears with a circle around it (◎), it is a *whole note* and lasts for 4 beats. When a number appears with a circle and a stem (♩), it is a *half note* and lasts for 2 beats. When a number appears with a stem only (♩), it is a *quarter note* and lasts for 1 beat. When a number appears with a stem and either a beam or a flag (♫ or ♪), it is an *eighth note* and lasts for one half of a beat. (Eighth notes are beamed when they are in groups of two or four; when by themselves, they appear with flags.)

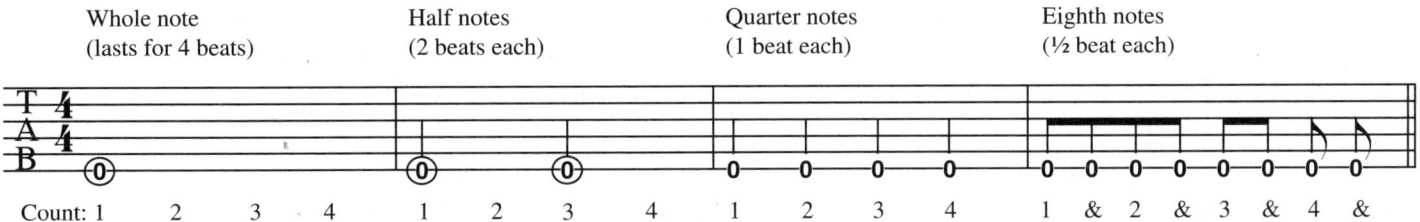

A rest is a silence that lasts for a certain amount of time. Each of the note values above has a corresponding rest value.

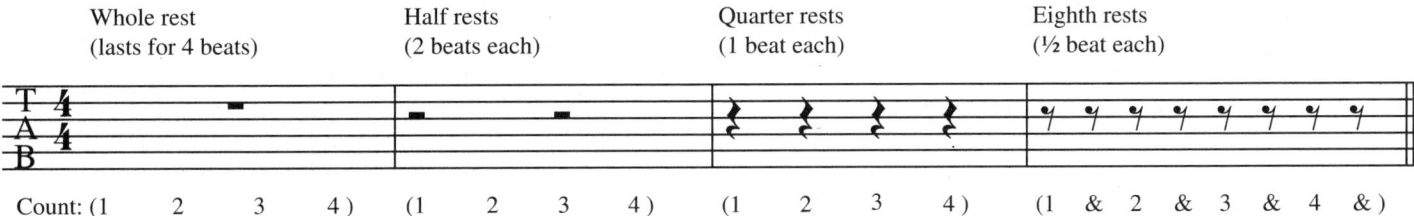

In the example above, notice that counting numbers for rests are in parentheses.

LESSON 2: RHYTHM EXERCISES

Just to make sure you have a grip on everything we just covered, let's try some rhythm exercises. We will be playing the open 6th string, using combinations of all the different note and rest values. Tap your foot to the rhythm and count the beats aloud. Be sure to listen to the CD to make sure you're getting the rhythms right.

Note: Remember, unless otherwise indicated, everything in this book should be played using downstrokes of the pick.

Whole Notes and Rests

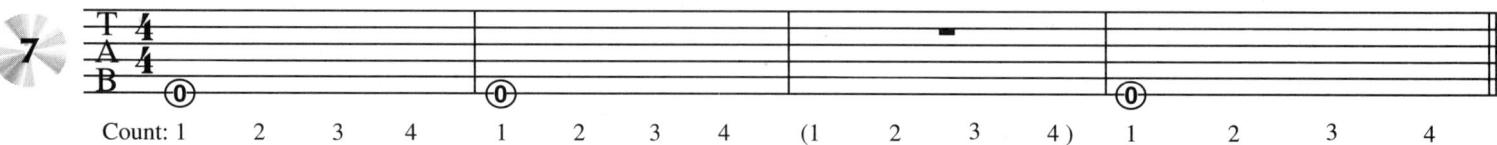

Half Notes and Rests

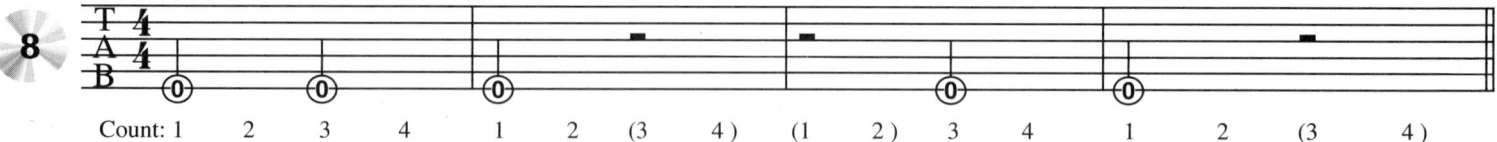

Quarter Notes and Rests

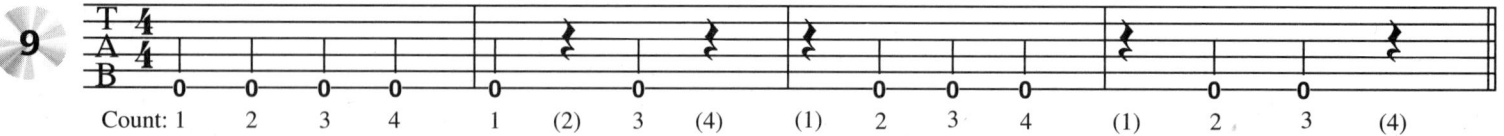

Eighth Notes and Rests

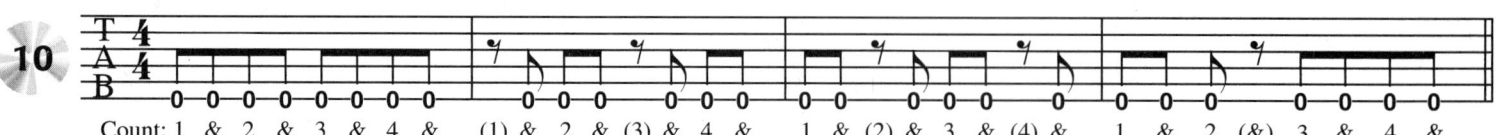

All Notes and Rests Combined 1

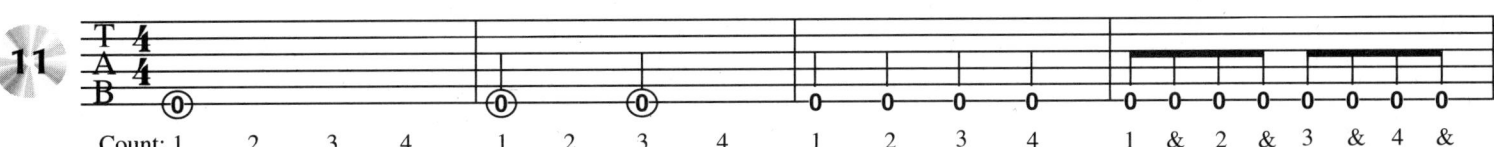

Count: 1   2   3   4   1   2   3   4   1   2   3   4   1 & 2 & 3 & 4 &

5

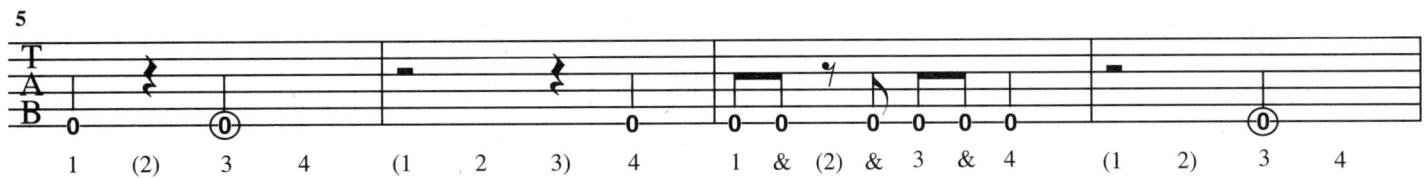

1   (2)   3   4   (1)   2   3)   4   1 & (2) & 3 & 4   (1)   2)   3   4

9

(1   2   3   4)   1   2   3   (4)   1 & (2)   3 & (4)   1   2   3   4

All Notes and Rests Combined 2

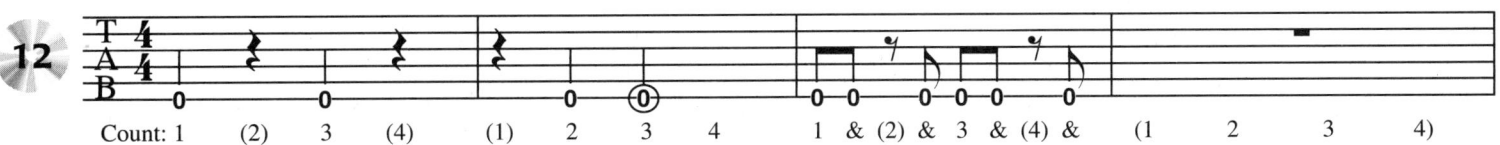

Count: 1   (2)   3   (4)   (1)   2   3   4   1 & (2) & 3 & (4) &   (1   2   3   4)

5

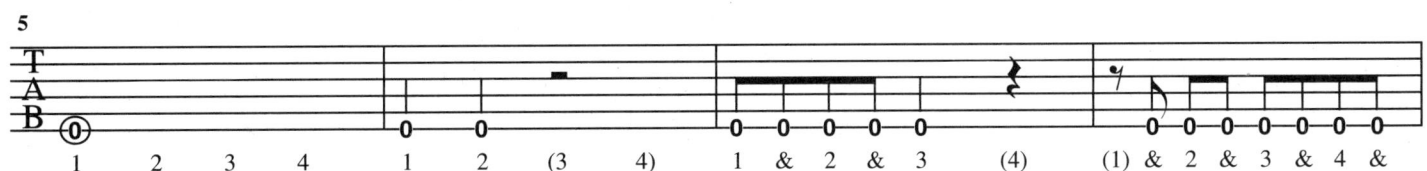

1   2   3   4   1   2   (3   4)   1 & 2 & 3   (4)   (1) & 2 & 3 & 4 &

9

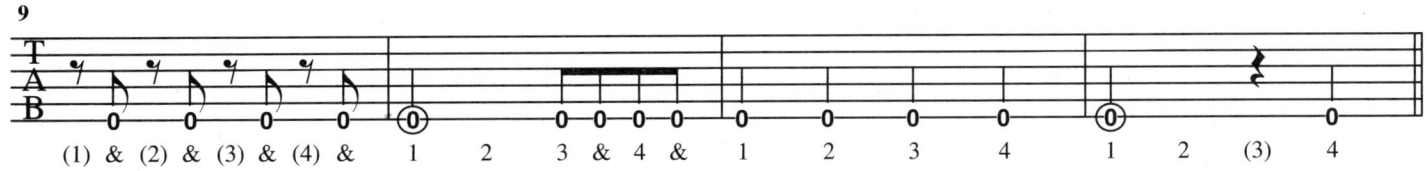

(1) & (2) & (3) & (4) &   1   2   3 & 4 &   1   2   3   4   1   2   (3)   4

LESSON 3: WARM-UPS

It's important to begin your practice sessions with some warm-ups. If you were doing any other kind of physical workout, you would probably warm up with some stretches before jumping into the "big weights."

The first warm-up is an exercise for your right hand, keeping in mind everything we covered about right-hand technique on page 16. You will be playing four quarter notes on each open string, first going up (6th, 5th, 4th, etc.), then going down (1st, 2nd, 3rd, etc.). Play the notes steadily and evenly, striving for a good, solid tone throughout. Keep in mind that the numbers under the TAB staff indicate which left-hand finger to use. If it is a "0," play the string open.

Warm-Up No. 1

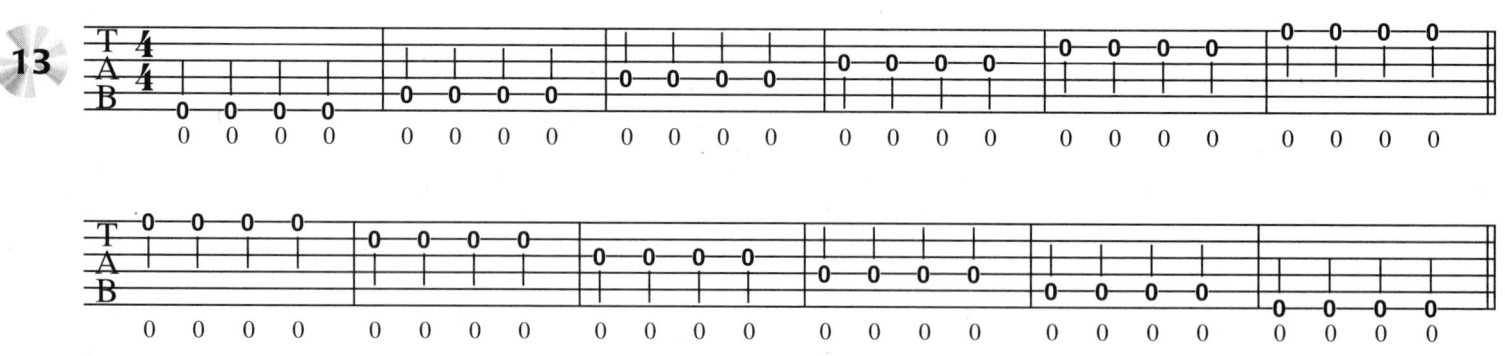

This next warm-up is the same as the one above, only played with eighth notes instead of quarter notes.

Warm-Up No. 2

Warm-Up No. 3 involves the right *and* left hands. Go back and review left-hand technique on page 16 if you need a refresher. Starting on the 6th string, play quarter notes on the 1st, 2nd, 3rd, and 4th frets. Do the same on the 5th string, 4th string, 3rd string, etc. Then, starting with the 1st string, go backwards—4th fret, 3rd, 2nd, 1st—all the way down through the 6th string. Again, the most important thing here is to play the notes steadily and evenly, striving for a good tone throughout (no fret buzz!).

Warm-Up No. 3

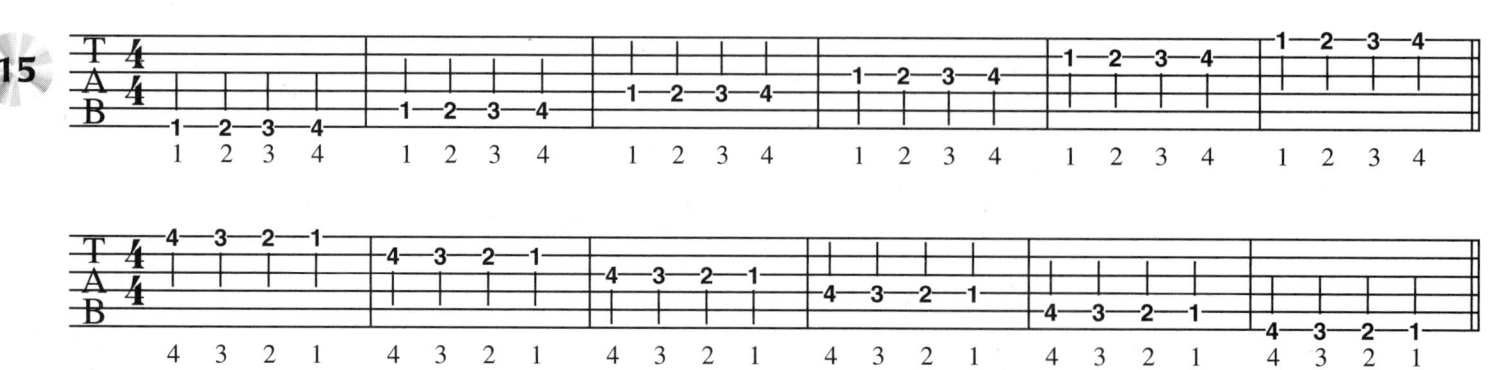

The following exercises isolate all of the possible left-hand finger combinations. Practice them all, especially Warm-Up No. 6, which features the 3rd/4th finger combo; this one can be very helpful in developing the pinky finger, which is a little weakling and just wants to ride the coattails of the ring finger.

Warm-Up No. 4

Warm-Up No. 5

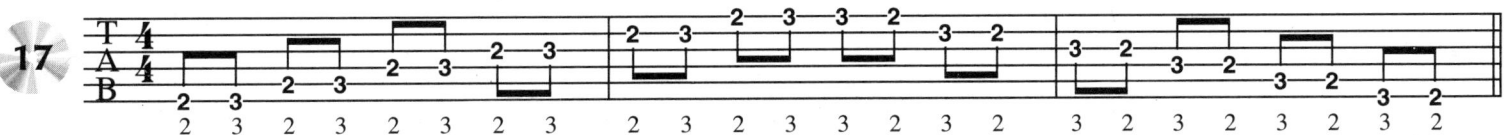

Warm-Up No. 6

Warm-Up No. 7

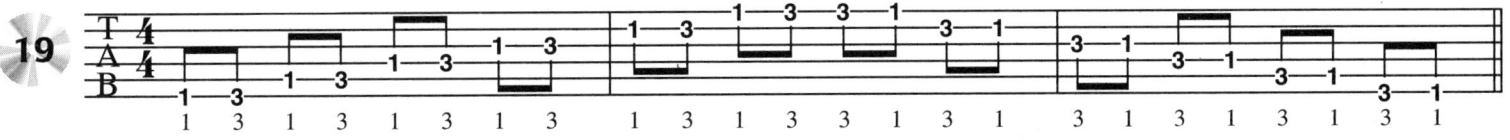

Warm-Up No. 8

Warm-Up No. 9

LESSON 4: SINGLE-STRING RIFFS

Now that you're all warmed up, it's time to play some music. Believe it or not, there are lots of cool riffs and songs that can be played using just one string. For the following examples, you will only be using the 6th string, which sounds great by itself. It has a thick, heavy tone, and if you have distortion on your amplifier (or as a separate foot pedal), you'll sound even heavier. Have fun with these examples in the styles of Led Zeppelin, The White Stripes, and Deep Purple. Listen to the accompanying CD to make sure you are getting the rhythms right.

Note: Most of the examples in this book have *repeat signs* (:||). A repeat sign tells you to go back to the beginning, or to a forward-facing repeat sign (||:), and repeat what you just played. If you see a "3x" or "4x" above the repeat sign, it means to repeat the section 3 or 4 times, respectively.

In the Style of "Babe I'm Gonna Leave You" by Led Zeppelin

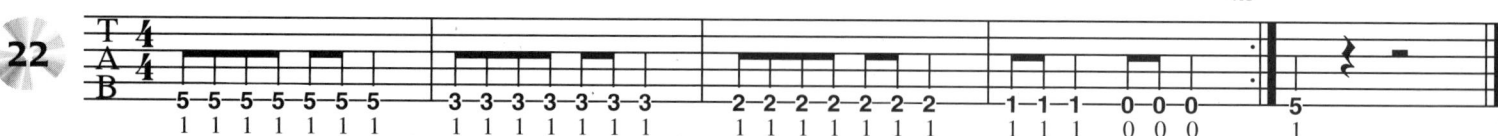

In the Style of "Seven Nation Army" by The White Stripes

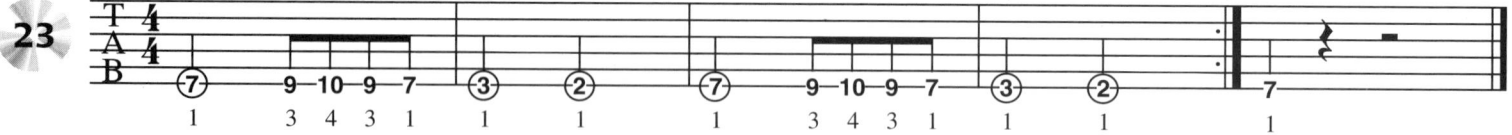

Jimmy Page (b. 1944) was the guitarist, co-songwriter, and producer for Led Zeppelin, one of the most successful and influential rock bands of all time. His heavy riffs, wild solos, and intense stage presence helped define what it means to be a rock guitarist. He combined his roots in the blues with other influences, such as folk, funk, and country, to create his innovative hard-rock style.

Ties

For the next song, you'll need to learn about *ties*. A tie is a curved line ⌣ that connects two notes of the same pitch. The tied notes last for the combined values of both notes. So, you would pick the first note and let it ring for the duration of both.

Check out the tie example below. Listen to the CD and make sure to count out the beats.

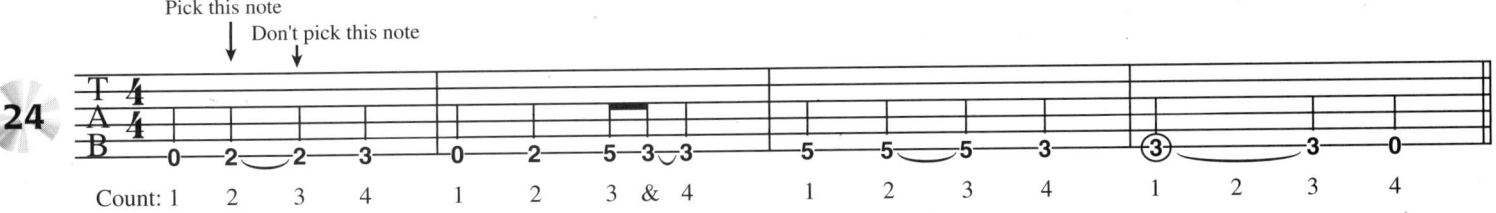

The next song is in the style of an all-time guitar classic. It is a rite of passage for beginning guitar players to learn Deep Purple's "Smoke on the Water." This is a longer example, so you have a chance to settle into the groove and jam along with the band on the CD.

In the Style of "Smoke on the Water" by Deep Purple

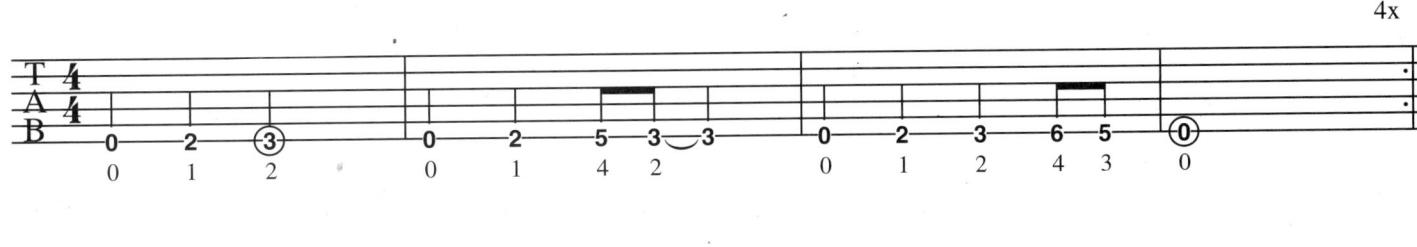

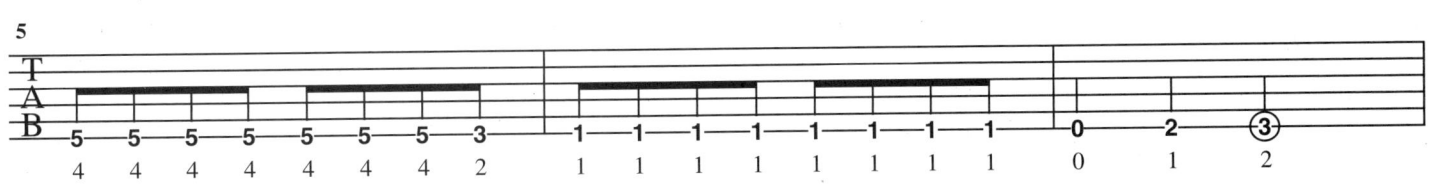

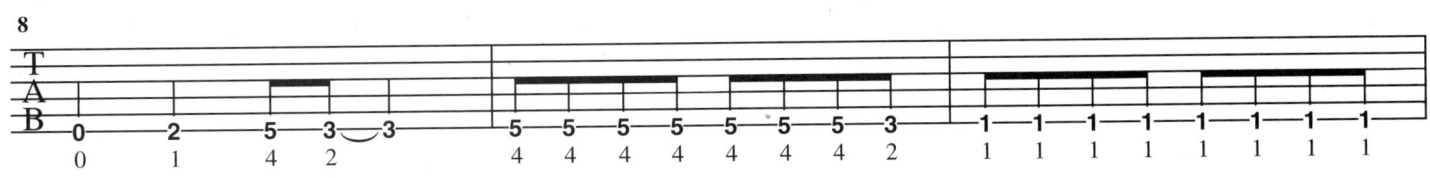

LESSON 5: OPEN POWER CHORDS

Now, we're going to fatten up our sound a bit by playing two strings at a time. Although, technically, a *chord* is defined as three or more notes played simultaneously, these two-string combos are known as *power chords.* They are the cornerstone of rock, blues, and lots of other types of music. A power chord consists of two notes: the *root,* which is the bottom note (and gives the chord its name) and the *5th* above it. Because of this 5th, power chords are also known as "5" chords (for instance, E5, C5, etc.). For this book, we don't really need to know what a 5th is, but we do need to know where to play it. The 5th is two frets higher than the root note on the next adjacent string.

For example, if our root note was on the open 6th string (E), the 5th would be on the 2nd fret of the 5th string. This is an E5 chord.

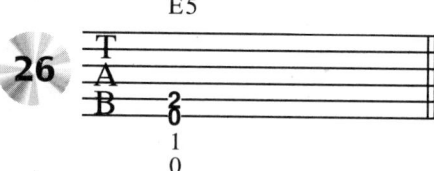

The chord above is an *open* power chord because one of its notes (in this case, the root note) is played on an open string. There are two more open power chords for you to learn in this lesson: A5 and D5.

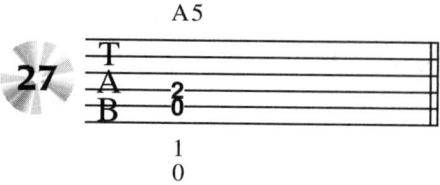

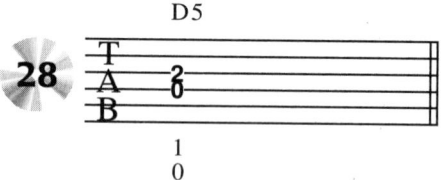

Some guitarists have built entire careers around playing these types of chords. The good news is they sound great and they're easy to play—just be careful to pick only the two notes in each chord. Give all three chords a try and then play the examples on the next page.

This first example is a straightforward, powerful rock groove.

Open Power Chord Exercise

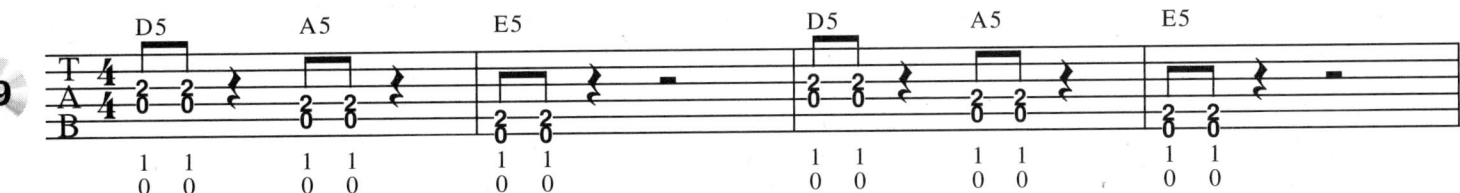

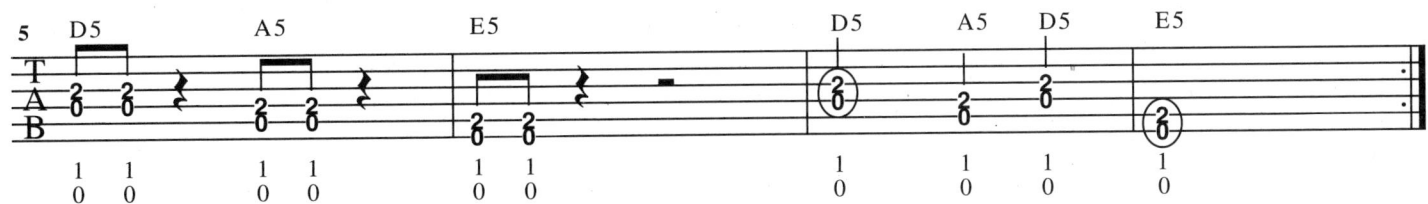

The next example is a lot of fun to hammer out, and it's in the style of one of the most famous punk bands of all time, The Clash.

In the Style of "Should I Stay or Should I Go" by The Clash

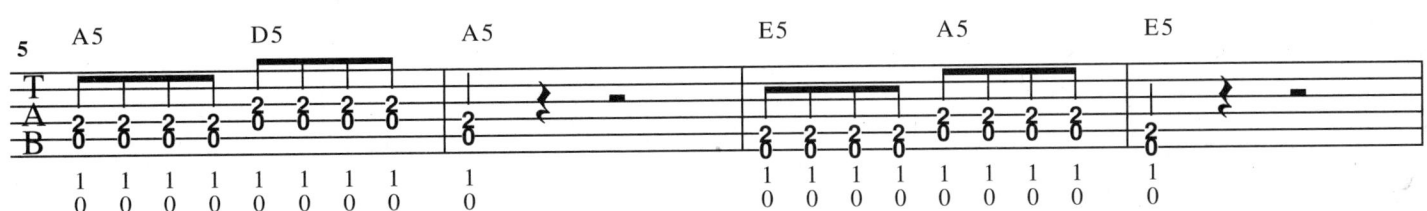

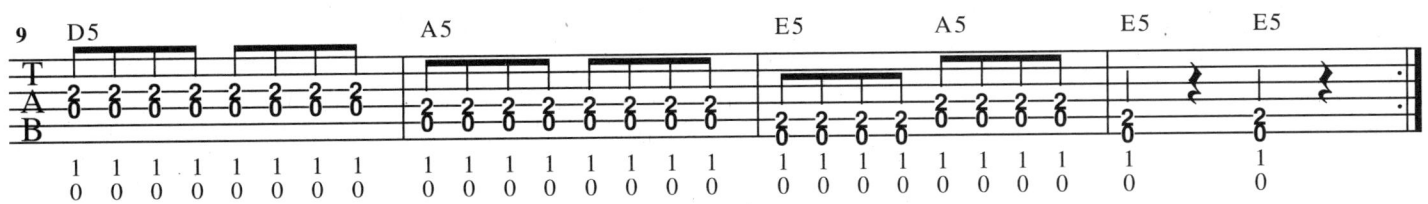

LESSON 6: PLAYING THE BLUES

In this lesson, we're going to embellish a bit on the open power chords we learned in the previous lesson. We are going to play patterns that start with these power chords, then replace the 5th with the note two frets higher. This new note is the *6th,* so we'll call these chords "6" chords (A6, D6, E6, etc.). We'll refer to the patterns themselves as *blues patterns* because they are an essential technique of blues guitar playing.

Our first pattern starts with the A5 power chord, then goes to A6 and alternates back and forth. Try it as many times as it takes for you to feel comfortable.

A Blues Pattern

The second pattern is exactly the same, but played on the next set of strings. It starts on the D5 power chord, then goes to D6.

D Blues Pattern

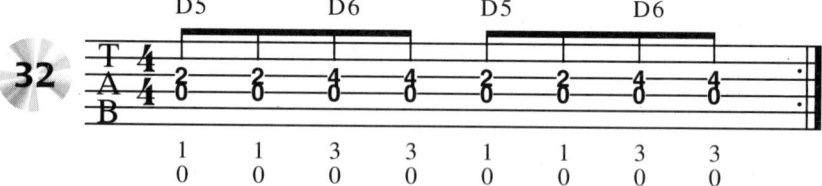

The third pattern starts on E5, then goes to E6.

E Blues Pattern

12-Bar Blues Progression

Now, we're going to put these patterns together and play the *12-bar blues progression.* A progression is a series of chords. This particular progression is used not only in the blues, but in rock, punk, country, jazz, and other types of music; it's a handy thing to know.

A basic 12-bar blues progression consists of 12 *bars,* or measures, and usually only three chords (in this case A5, D5, and E5). First, we'll play the progression using just the open power chords.

Note: On the CD, you will hear two versions of the following two examples. First, you will hear them played with a *straight* rhythm (Tracks 34 and 36), then you will hear them played with a *swing,* or *shuffle,* rhythm (Tracks 35 and 37). The straight rhythm is the rhythmic feel you've been using so far. The swing rhythm has a kind of "skipping" feel to the eighth notes: long-short-long-short, long-short-long-short, etc. Listen to the CD and play along to really get the feel of the swing rhythm.

12-Bar Blues Progression

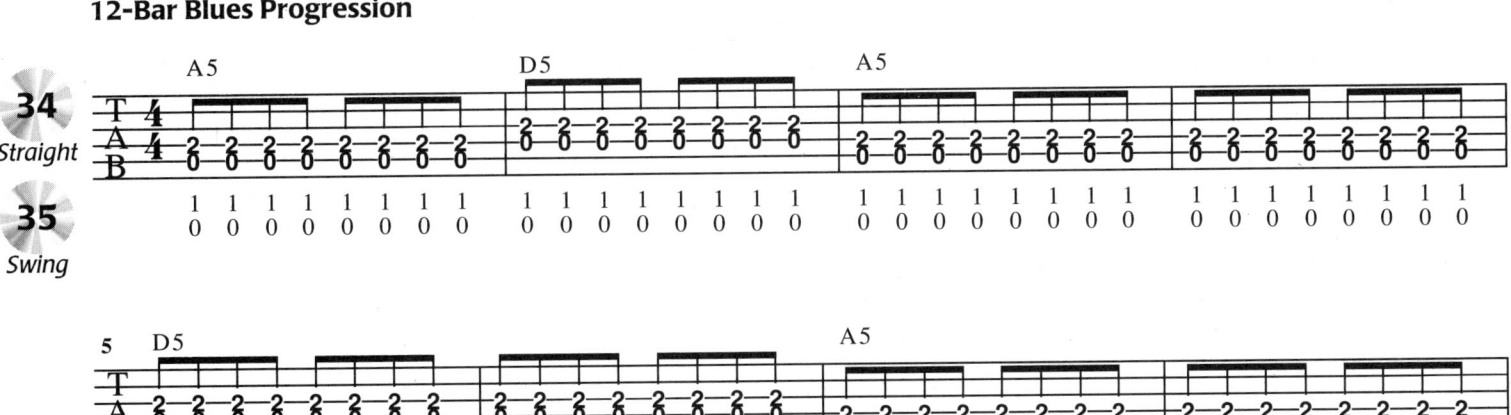

Now, let's play the 12-bar blues progression using the patterns we learned on the previous page.

12-Bar Blues Progression (Using Blues Patterns)

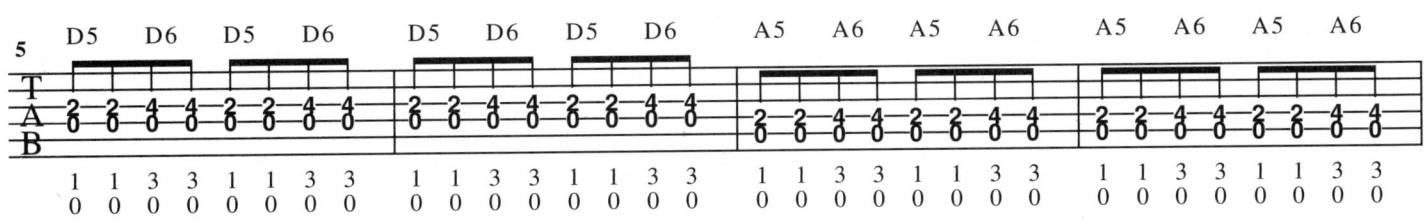

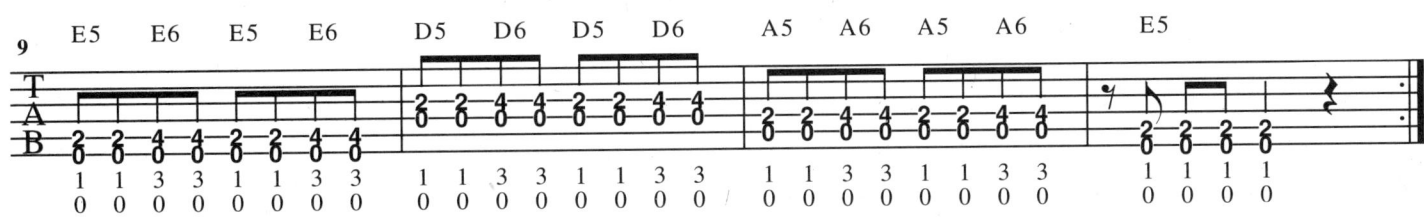

LESSON 7: MOVEABLE POWER CHORDS

So far, we've only looked at open power chords, which use open strings. Now, we'll look at *moveable,* or *closed position,* power chords that are made up of only fretted notes. This chord form is so amazing because it can be moved up and down the fretboard to create all kinds of great riffs. Many guitarists have made their fortunes by writing songs using just this one chord form.

Root-6 Power Chords

The first type of moveable power chord we'll look at is the *root-6* power chord. It's called a "root-6" power chord because its root note is on the 6th string. (See illustration to the right. This is a *chord diagram,* which shows how a chord is fingered on the fretboard.)

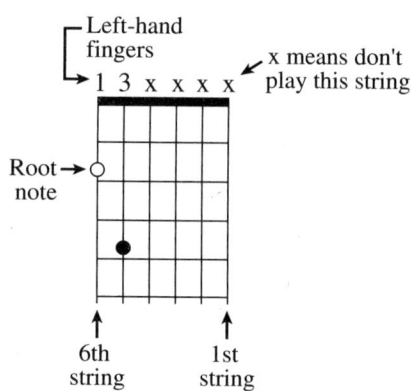

The great thing about a moveable power chord is that you can move it to any fret on the guitar and it becomes a new chord. For instance, place the chord form with the root note at the 3rd fret (the G note) and you have a G5 chord. Place the chord form with the root note at the 5th fret (A) and you get A5. Place the root note at the 10th fret (D) and you get D5, etc. (Refer to the fretboard chart on page 47 to see the note names for every fret of every string on the guitar.) Let's try these moveable power chords.

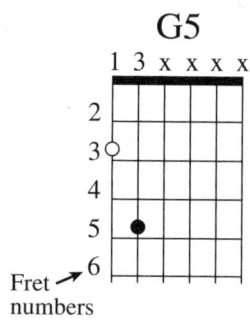

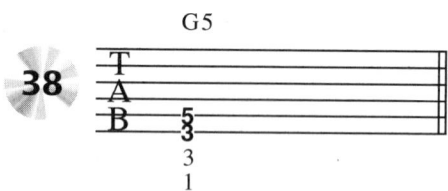

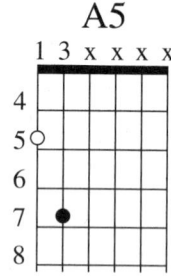

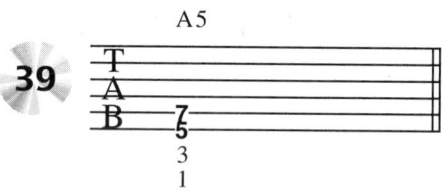

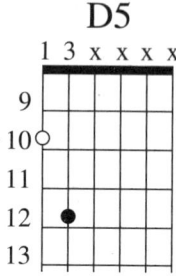

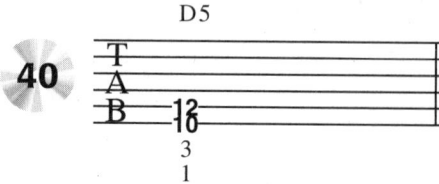

In most cases in this book, the chord names will not appear above the power chords (like above); too much information might be confusing at this point. It will suffice to notate the power chords in TAB only.

Now, let's try a few examples using moveable power chords. The first one is in the style of the final section of Led Zeppelin's epic "Stairway to Heaven." It features a common chord progression used in tons of rock tunes. Turn up the volume and distortion for this one.

In the Style of "Stairway to Heaven" by Led Zeppelin

The following example is in the style of a couple of great tunes: "You Really Got Me" by The Kinks and "N.I.B." by Black Sabbath. This is a simple riff that is a lot of fun to play. Like all of the examples in this book, play it as many times as you want—don't stop with just one repeat. Play it over and over again until you get in the groove and it starts to feel good.

In the Style of "You Really Got Me" by The Kinks and "N.I.B." by Black Sabbath

We already played this next example as a single-string riff (page 24). It features another common rock progression used in songs like "Babe I'm Gonna Leave You" by Led Zeppelin and "25 or 6 to 4" by Chicago. Notice the heavier sound when you play this using power chords instead of a single string, and watch out for the open power chord in measure 4.

In the Style of "Babe I'm Gonna Leave You" by Led Zeppelin

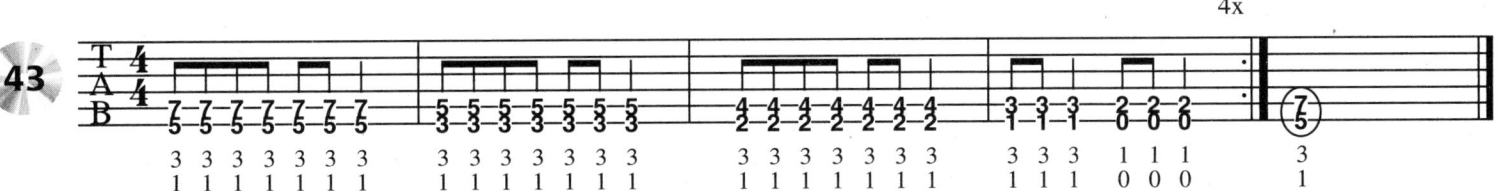

Root-5 Power Chords

Now, we'll look at *root-5* power chords, which are exactly like root-6 power chords except their root notes are on the 5th string.

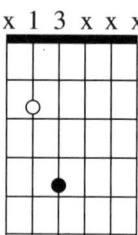

Like the root-6 power chord, you can move it to any fret and it becomes a new chord. For instance, if you place the chord form with the root note at the 3rd fret (C), you get a C5 chord. If you place the chord form with the root note at the 5th fret (D), you get D5. If you place the root note at the 10th fret (G), you get G5, etc. (Again, you may refer to the fretboard chart on page 47 to see the note names for every fret of every string on the guitar.) Now, let's try these root-5 power chords.

C5

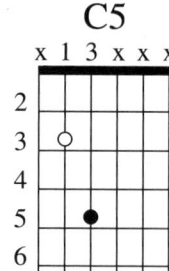

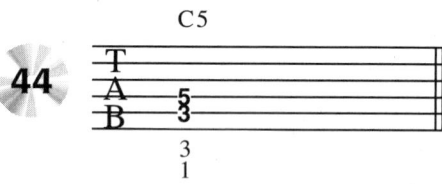

D5

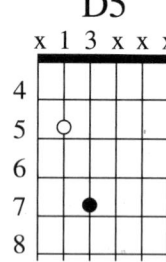

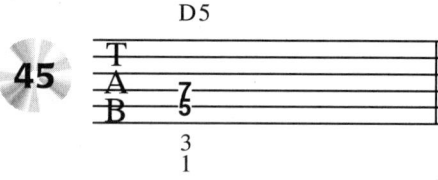

G5

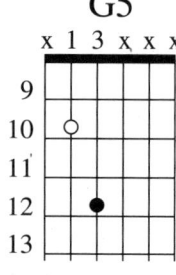

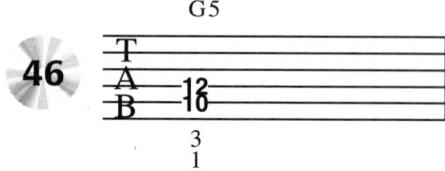

Again, for easier reading, we will not include root-5 power chord names in the examples that follow; the TAB will suffice.

Now, let's try a couple of examples using moveable root-5 power chords. The following is similar to Track 43 on page 31. It features the same type of chord progression except with root-5 power chords. Like Track 43, this progression descends the fretboard to an open power chord. For that crisp Green Day sound, make sure you attack the chords sharply, cutting them off completely during the rests. This will create a strong, driving rhythm.

In the Style of "Brain Stew" by Green Day

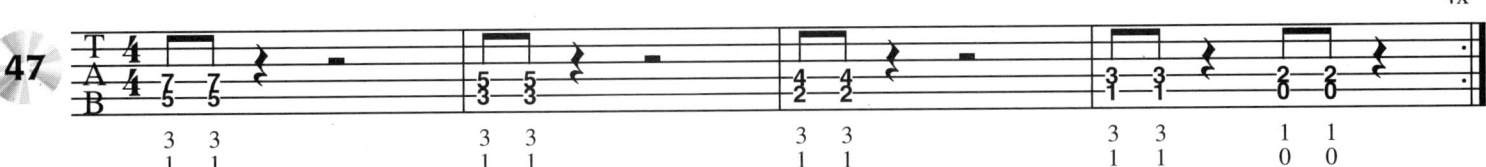

The next example also combines moveable and open power chords. In addition, you will deviate from the power-chord formula in measures 5–8. In measures 5 and 6, you will alternate between an open power chord and a *double stop* (two notes played at the same time), in which you leave your 1st finger on the 2nd fret of the 4th string, move your 2nd finger to the 3rd fret of the 6th string, and play the two notes simultaneously. Be careful here to block the 5th string with the pad of your 2nd finger while it is fretting the 6th string (you do not want to hear the 5th string ringing out on this double stop). In measures 7 and 8, you will start with a power chord, then remove your 1st finger from the root, creating a new double stop, then repeat this pattern. This is in the style of another Zeppelin classic.

In the Style of "Good Times, Bad Times" by Led Zeppelin

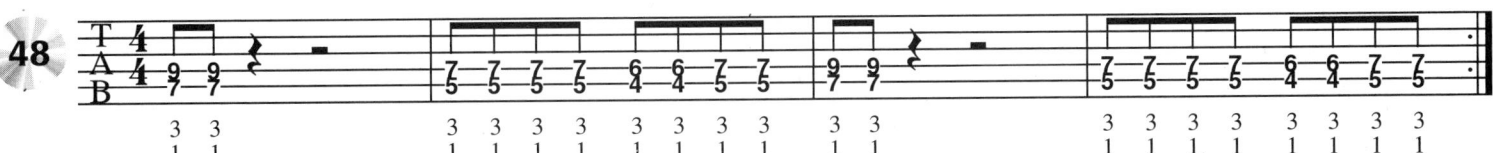

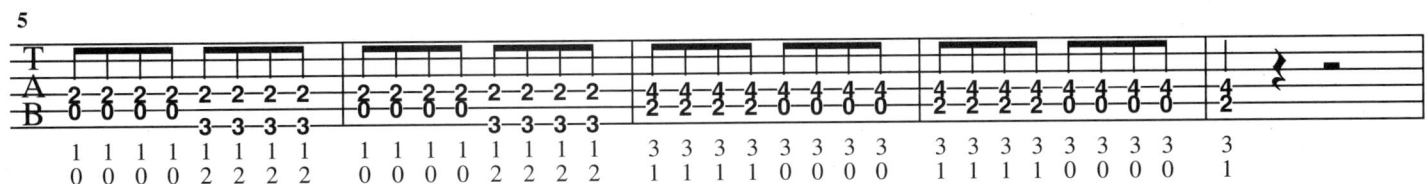

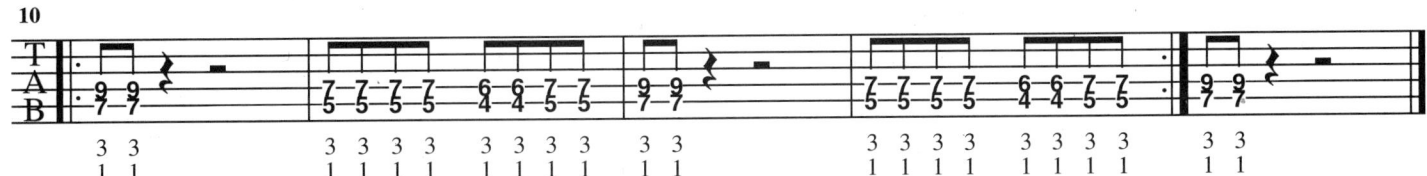

LESSON 8: MULTIPLE-STRING RIFFS

Remember (page 24), we learned that we could play cool-sounding riffs on just one string? Well, now we're going to play single-note riffs on multiple strings. In other words, we'll be picking individual notes, but on more than one string.

In the following example, certain notes should be held so that they ring out while you're playing other notes. In measure 1, hold your 1st finger on the first note while you play the rest of the notes in the measure. Do the same thing for measures 2, 4, and 5. This will produce a smooth and flowing sound. Notes that should be held in this way are marked with an asterisk (∗) in the music. Try the examples on this page with a clean sound (no distortion) and a chorus effect (if you have one).

In the Style of "One" by Metallica

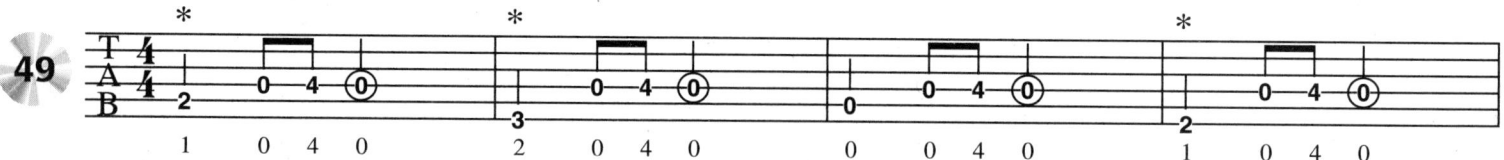

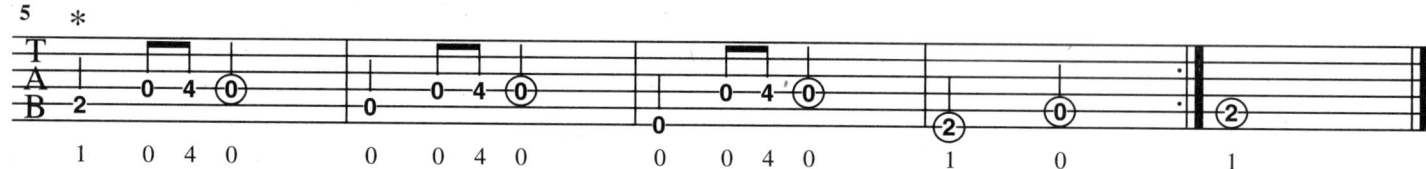

The next two examples also have notes that must be held while other notes are played.

In the Style of "Come as You Are" by Nirvana

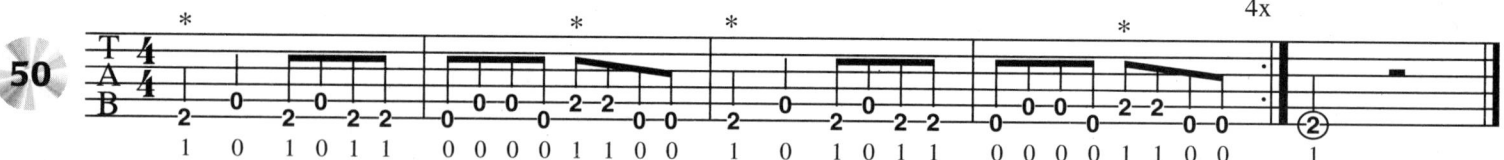

In the Style of "Don't Fear the Reaper" by Blue Öyster Cult

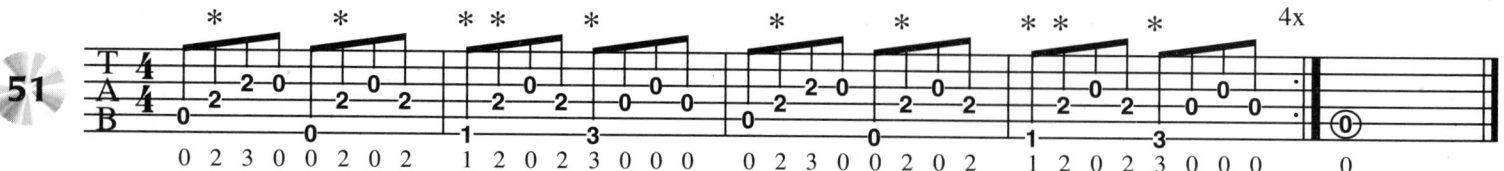

At first, the next example might appear to have a tricky rhythm, but if you listen to the CD, you'll see that it's quite easy. The time signature alternates between $\frac{3}{4}$ and $\frac{4}{4}$. We've already played lots of examples in $\frac{4}{4}$, and $\frac{3}{4}$ just means there are three beats per measure. Before you try the riff, it might be helpful to try counting: 1-2-3, 1-2-3-4, 1-2-3, 1-2-3-4, etc. Also, this example uses the swing rhythm we talked about on page 28.

In the Style of "Money" by Pink Floyd

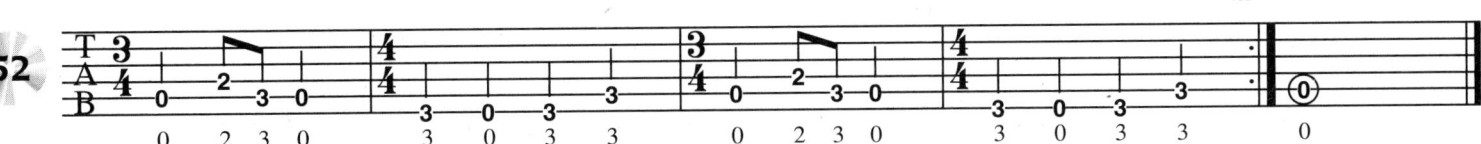

Now, we get to a song passed on by generations of electric guitar teachers (well, maybe just one long generation). This example is in the style of the intro to Ozzy Osbourne's "Crazy Train." You're going to be using your left-hand pinky for this one, so, hopefully, you've been keeping up with the exercises covered in the beginning of this book!

In the Style of "Crazy Train" by Ozzy Osbourne

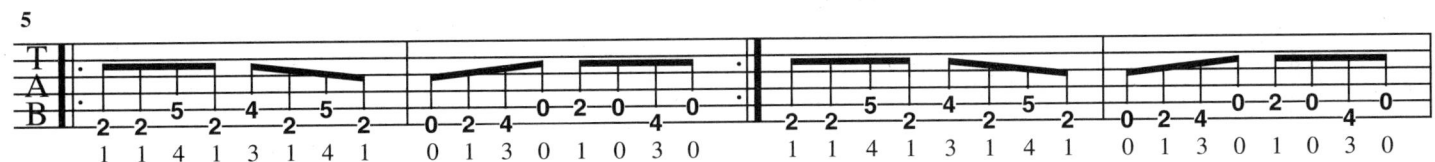

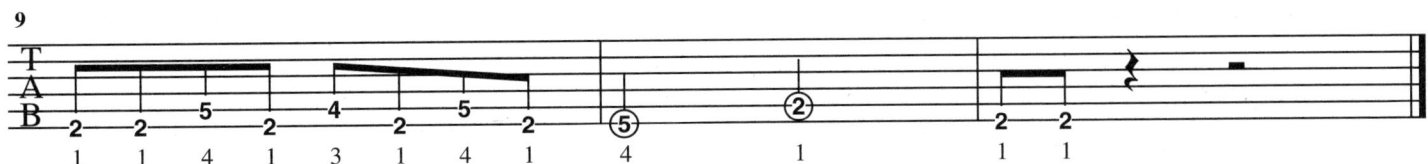

LESSON 9: THE PENTATONIC SCALE

In this lesson, we'll play single-note, multiple-string riffs based on the *pentatonic scale*. This is another powerful tool used by musicians for centuries. However, its secret powers were never truly revealed until it was invoked by the strings of an electric guitar.

E Minor Pentatonic Scale

A *scale* is a series of consecutive notes in a particular pattern. A *pentatonic scale* is a five-tone scale (*penta* means "five"). At this point, we don't need to delve into the theory behind the scale—we just need to know how to play it. Following is an E Minor Pentatonic scale. Like all scales, it's named after the first note, in this case E. In the example below, you may notice that there are six notes rather than five. The sixth note is just the *octave* of the first, meaning it has the same name but is located in a different *register,* or pitch range. Let's try the scale slowly, first ascending, then descending. Be sure to memorize this important scale.

E Minor Pentatonic Scale

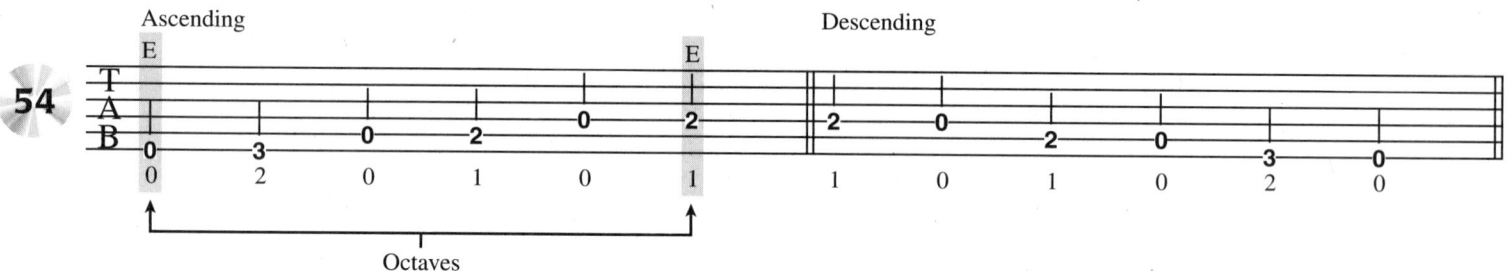

Dots

For the next couple of examples, you'll also need to learn about *dots*. When a dot follows a note (**0·**), its value is increased by one half. In other words, a dotted quarter note is the same as a quarter note tied to an eighth note (one-and-a-half beats).

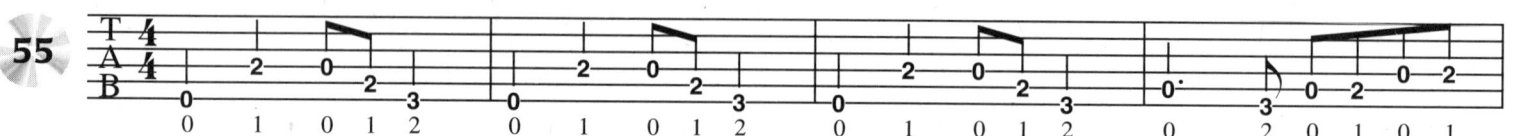

Following is a riff based on the E Minor Pentatonic scale. Notice that we end on a power chord for a strong finish. Also, watch out for the dotted quarter notes in measures 4 and 8. After you play this example, try making your own riffs using the notes of the E Minor Pentatonic scale—the possibilities are endless.

In the Style of Rage Against the Machine

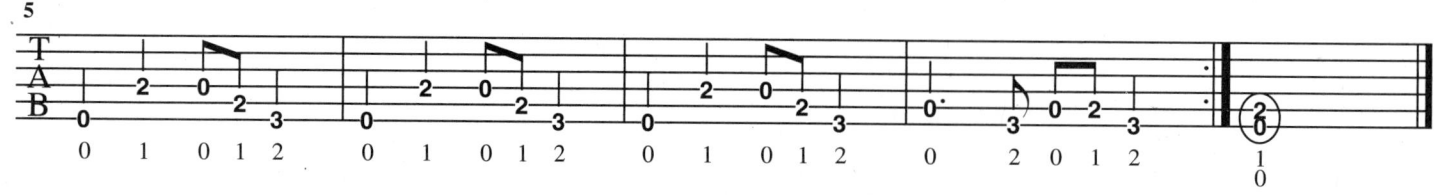

A Minor Pentatonic Scale

Now, we're going to look at the A Minor Pentatonic scale, which is a five-note scale starting on the open A string. Again, play it slowly going up, then going down. This scale should also be memorized. Don't waste any time. Do it now.

A Minor Pentatonic Scale

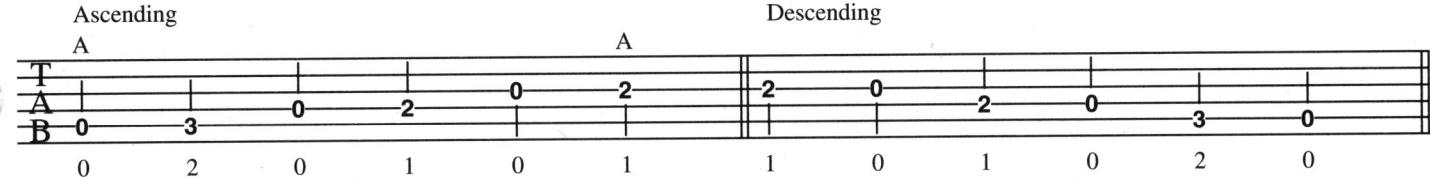

The tune below consists entirely of notes from the A Minor Pentatonic scale. It's in the style of "Voodoo Child (Slight Return)" by Jimi Hendrix, who was a master of the pentatonic scale among many other things. This is a great tune for breaking in a new wah-wah pedal. Like the example on the previous page, this song ends with a power chord. Watch out for the dotted notes in measures 1, 3, 5, and 7.

In the Style of "Voodoo Child (Slight Return)" by Jimi Hendrix

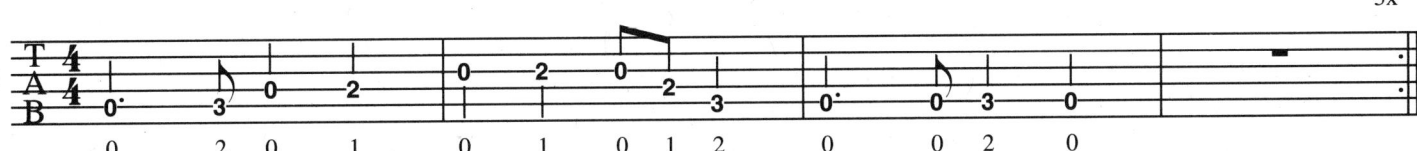

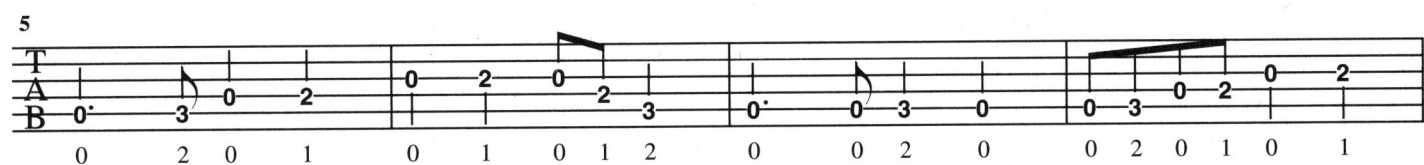

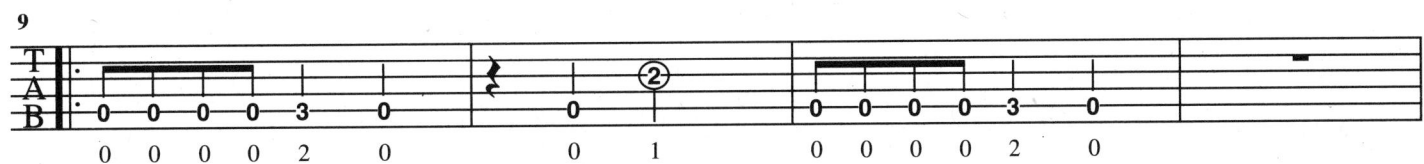

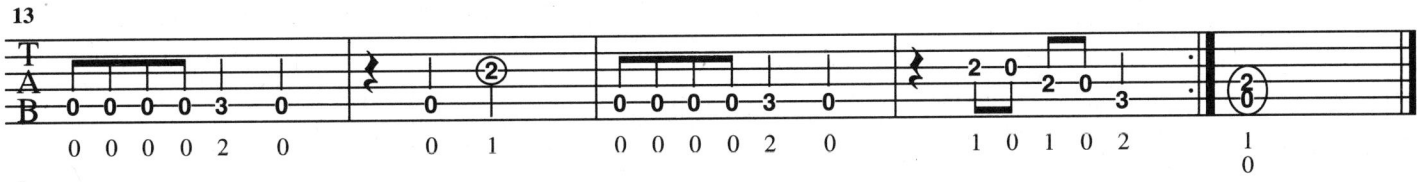

E Minor and A Minor Pentatonic Riffs Combined

Different scales can be combined in one song. Our next tune is made up of riffs based on both the E Minor and A Minor Pentatonic scales. Before we can play it, though, we need to talk about *sixteenth notes* and *hammer-ons.*

Sixteenth Notes

Sixteenth notes are beamed together with two beams () and last for one quarter of a beat each. In other words, it takes four sixteenth notes to equal one beat. Sixteenth notes are counted: 1-e-&-a, 2-e-&-a, 3-e-&-a, 4-e-&-a, etc.

Following are some exercises to get you used to playing sixteenth notes. Practice them slowly at first, maintaining a steady tempo. When they start to feel comfortable, try increasing the speed. Also, be sure to count the rhythms aloud while playing these exercises.

Sixteenth-Note Exercise No. 1

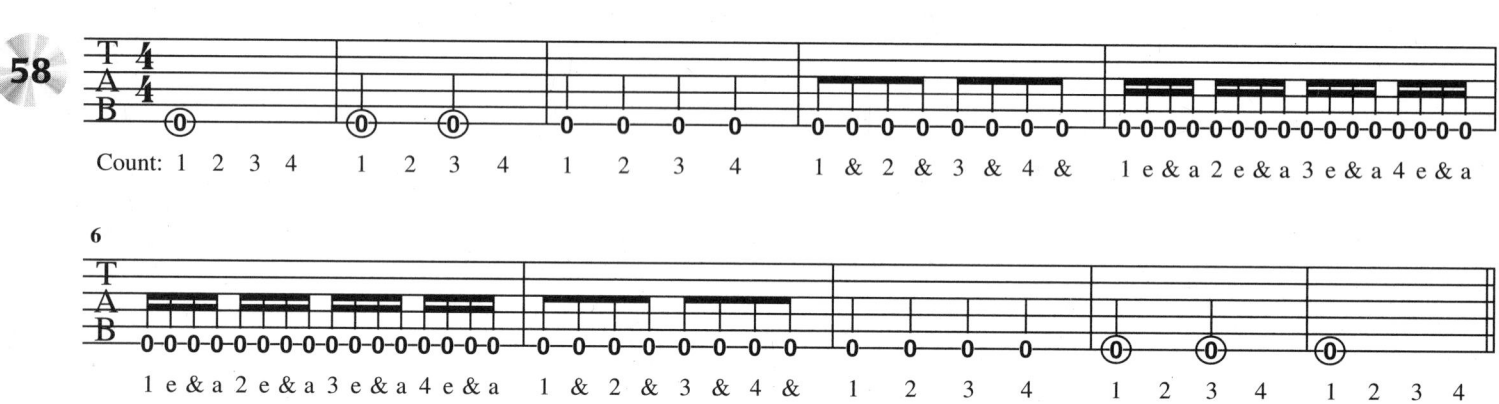

Sixteenth-Note Exercise No. 2

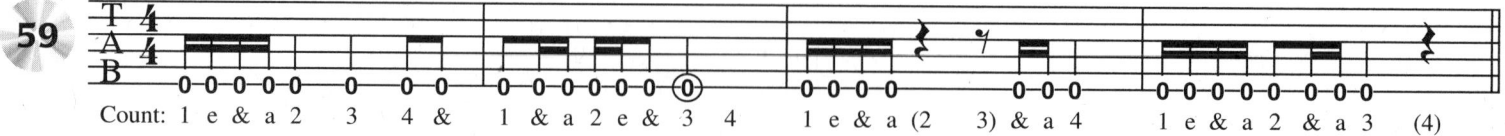

Sixteenth-Note Exercise No. 3

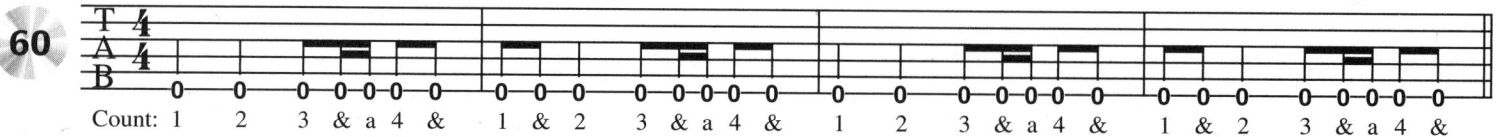

38

Hammer-Ons

A *hammer-on* is a cool technique you can use to give your riffs a more smooth, fluid feel. To play a hammer-on, pick a note, then forcefully bring a left-hand finger down onto a higher note on the same string, thereby causing the second note to sound. This "hammering" motion produces the sound—no picking is necessary on the second note. Below is an example of a hammer-on. Try it out. Play the 6th string open, then forcefully bring down your 2nd finger on the 2nd fret of the 6th string.

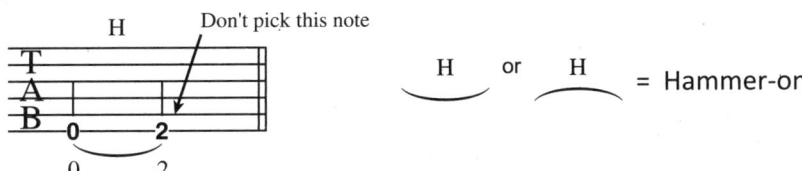

This technique can be challenging at first, especially when trying to keep the volume equal between the two notes. Try this next exercise, which consists of the E Minor and A Minor Pentatonic scales played with hammer-ons.

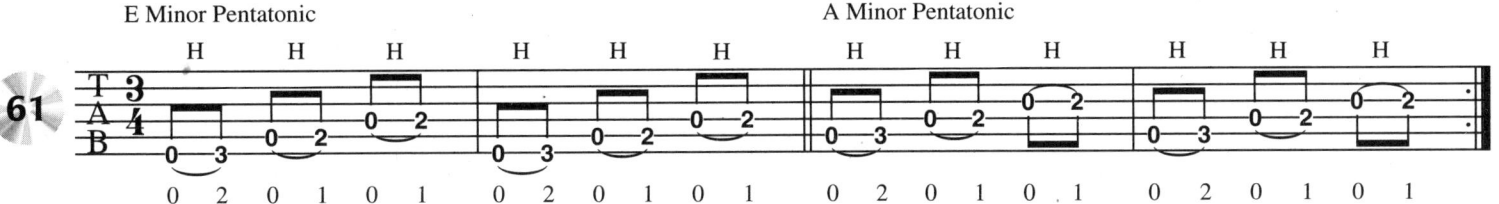

The next tune features sixteenth notes, hammer-ons, and a combination of E Minor and A Minor Pentatonic riffs.

In the Style of "Heartbreaker" by Led Zeppelin

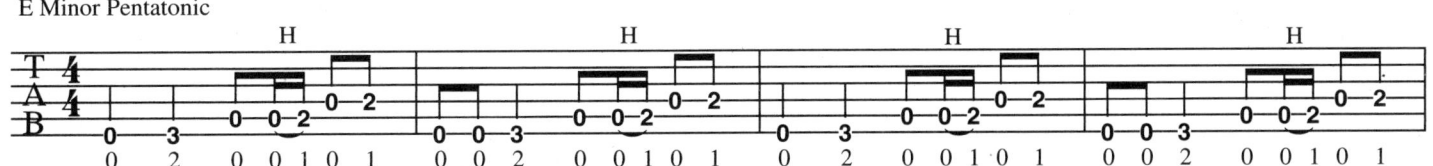

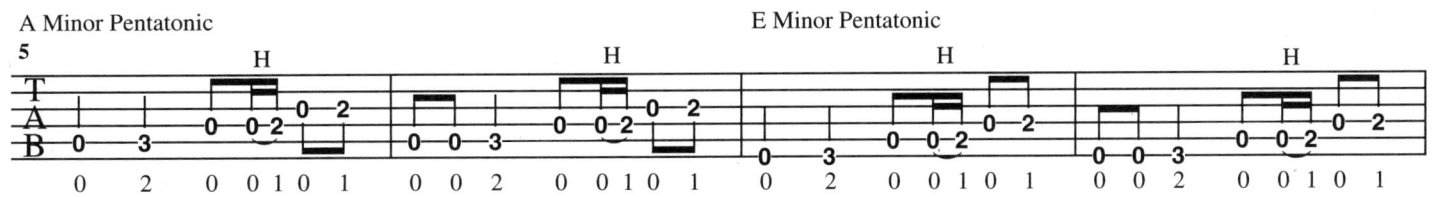

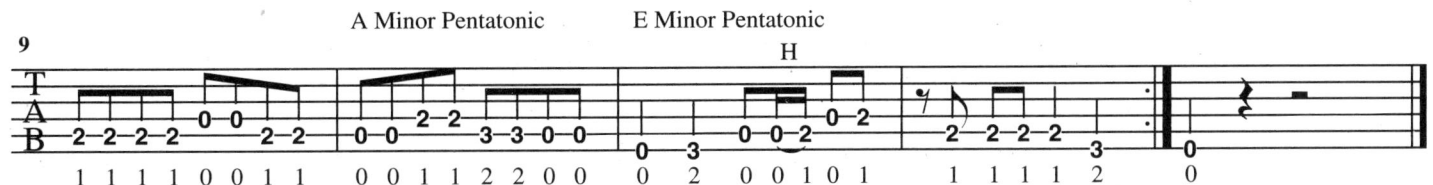

LESSON 10: RIFFS COMBINING ROOT-6 AND ROOT-5 POWER CHORDS

It's time to get back to our power chords. Now, we're going to combine root-6 and root-5 power chords in a single riff.

To get used to switching back and forth, try the following exercise. After playing the first power chord, lift your fingers up off the fretboard while maintaining the form of the chord in the air. Then, move them to the next set of adjacent strings, place them back on the fretboard, and play the next power chord. Go back and forth between the root-6 and root-5 power chords until you are comfortable.

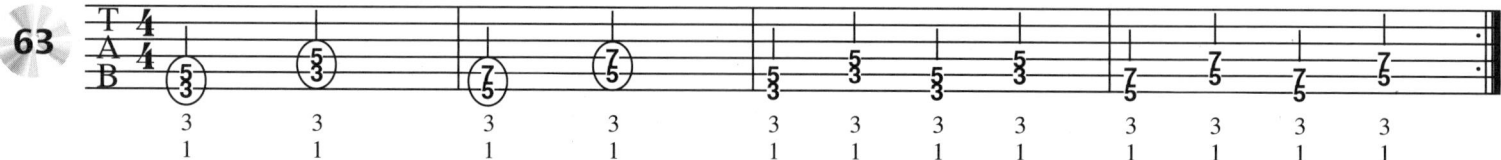

Now, let's try a fairly easy riff. This one's in the style of the tune that brought the Seattle grunge scene to the masses, Nirvana's "Smells Like Teen Spirit."

In the Style of "Smells Like Teen Spirit" by Nirvana

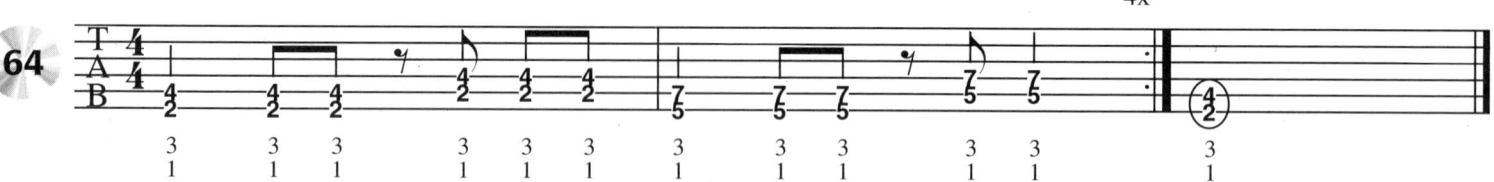

The chords jump around a bit more in the example below, so this one may take a little more practice.

In the Style of "Godzilla" by Blue Öyster Cult

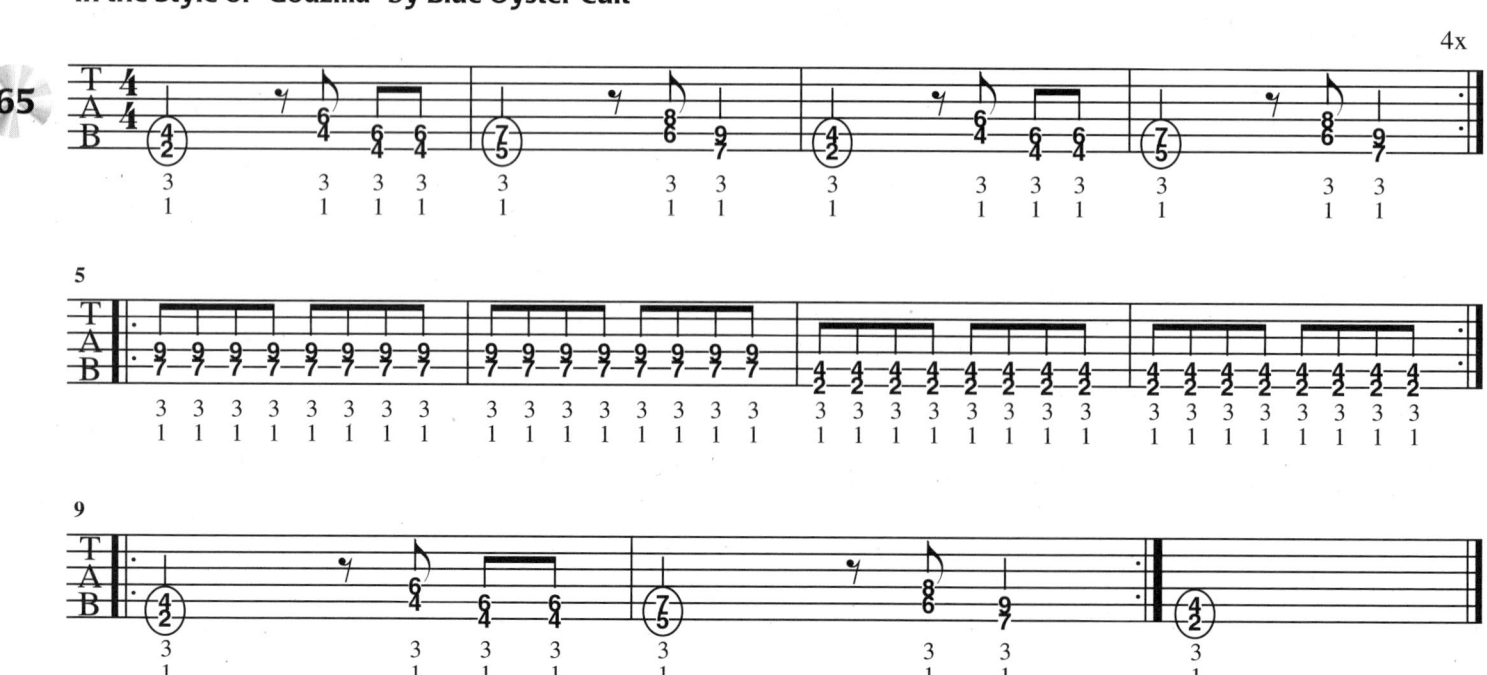

The next example features a root-5 power chord at the 7th fret. When playing this chord (which happens to be an E5), you can also include the open 6th string (low E) because it is the root note, just in a lower octave. The open string gives some additional weight to this power chord. We also snuck in an E Minor Pentatonic run in measure 12. (Lesson 11 features more examples that combine power chords with single-note riffs.)

In the Style of "Man in the Box" **by Alice in Chains**

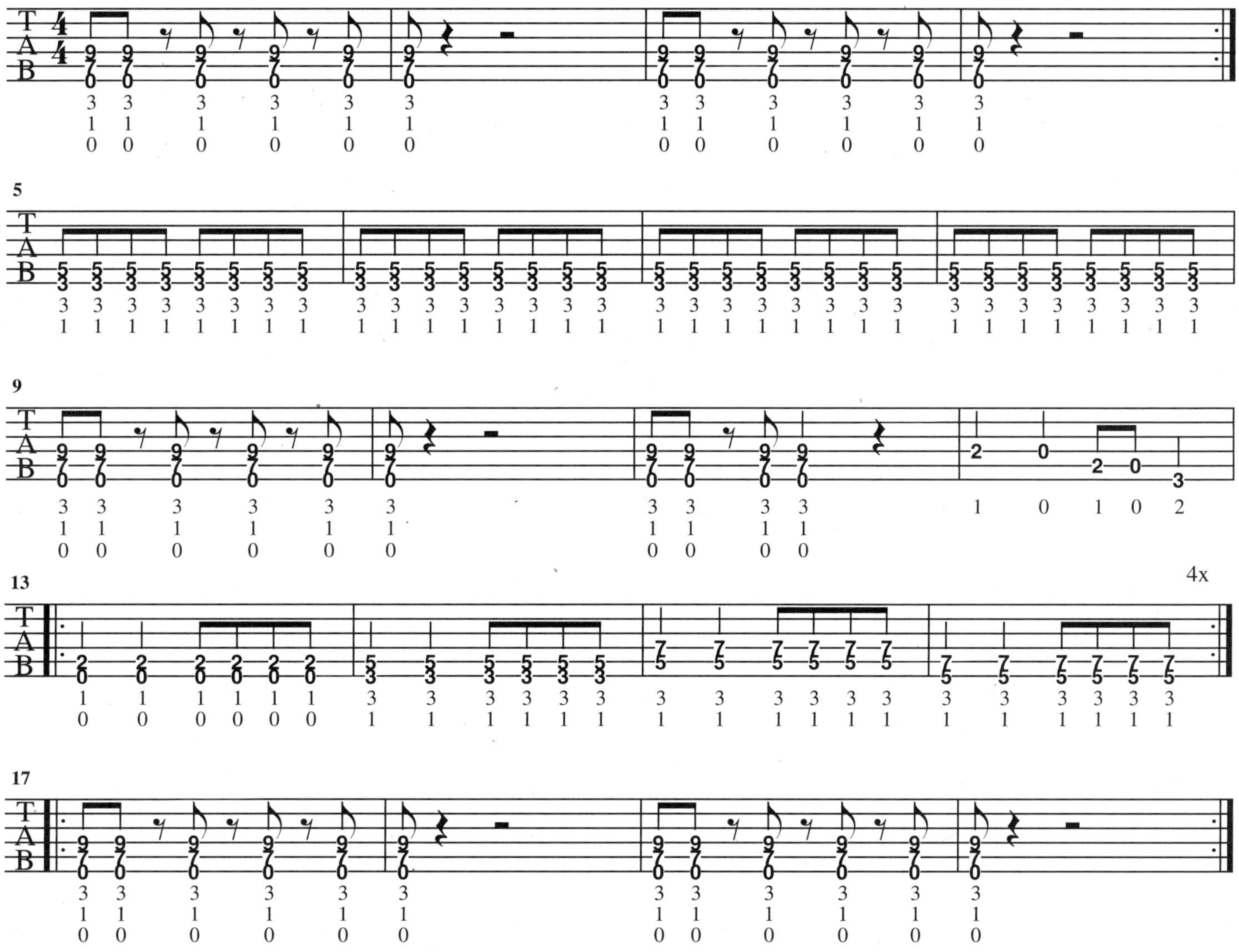

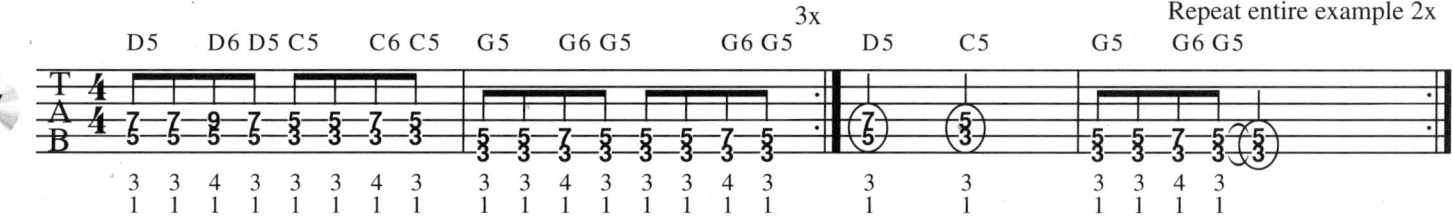

This next one, in the style of Warren Zevon's "Werewolves of London," uses root-5 and root-6 power chords, but it also features a pattern similar to the blues pattern introduced on page 28. The only difference is that on the "&" of every second and fourth beat, you return to the power chord instead of remaining on the 6 chord. (We will include chord names in this example to more clearly demonstrate the pattern.)

In the Style of "Werewolves of London" **by Warren Zevon**

LESSON 11: COMBINING POWER CHORDS WITH SINGLE-NOTE RIFFS

Now, we're going to combine power chords (root-6, root-5, open position, and moveable) and single-note riffs on multiple strings. This is the point where you really start sounding like you know a little something.

The first example features open power chords and an E Minor Pentatonic lick in measure 4. Although we didn't cover this scale on the upper strings, if you combine these notes with those covered on page 36, you will have a two-octave E Minor Pentatonic scale. This example is in the style of another all-time guitar classic.

Note: You can play the following two examples using only downstrokes. However, there are passages that might be easier to play using a technique called *alternate picking.* This is where you alternate between downstrokes (∏) and upstrokes (V) of the pick. These passages are indicated in the examples below.

In the Style of "Back in Black" by AC/DC

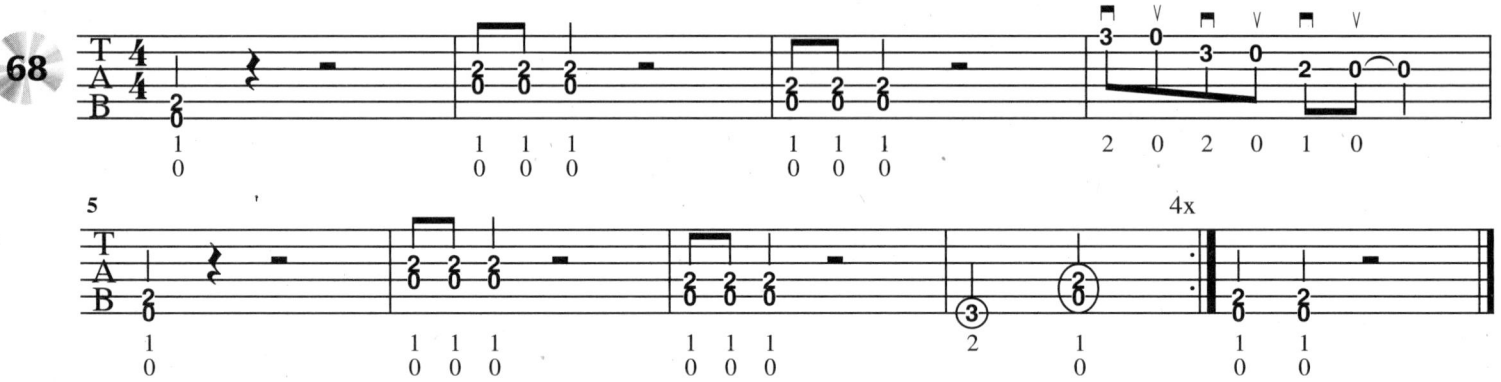

This next one is a little tricky, but it sounds great. Watch out for the time changes in measures 4, 5, 12, 13, 16, and 17.

In the Style of "The Ocean" by Led Zeppelin

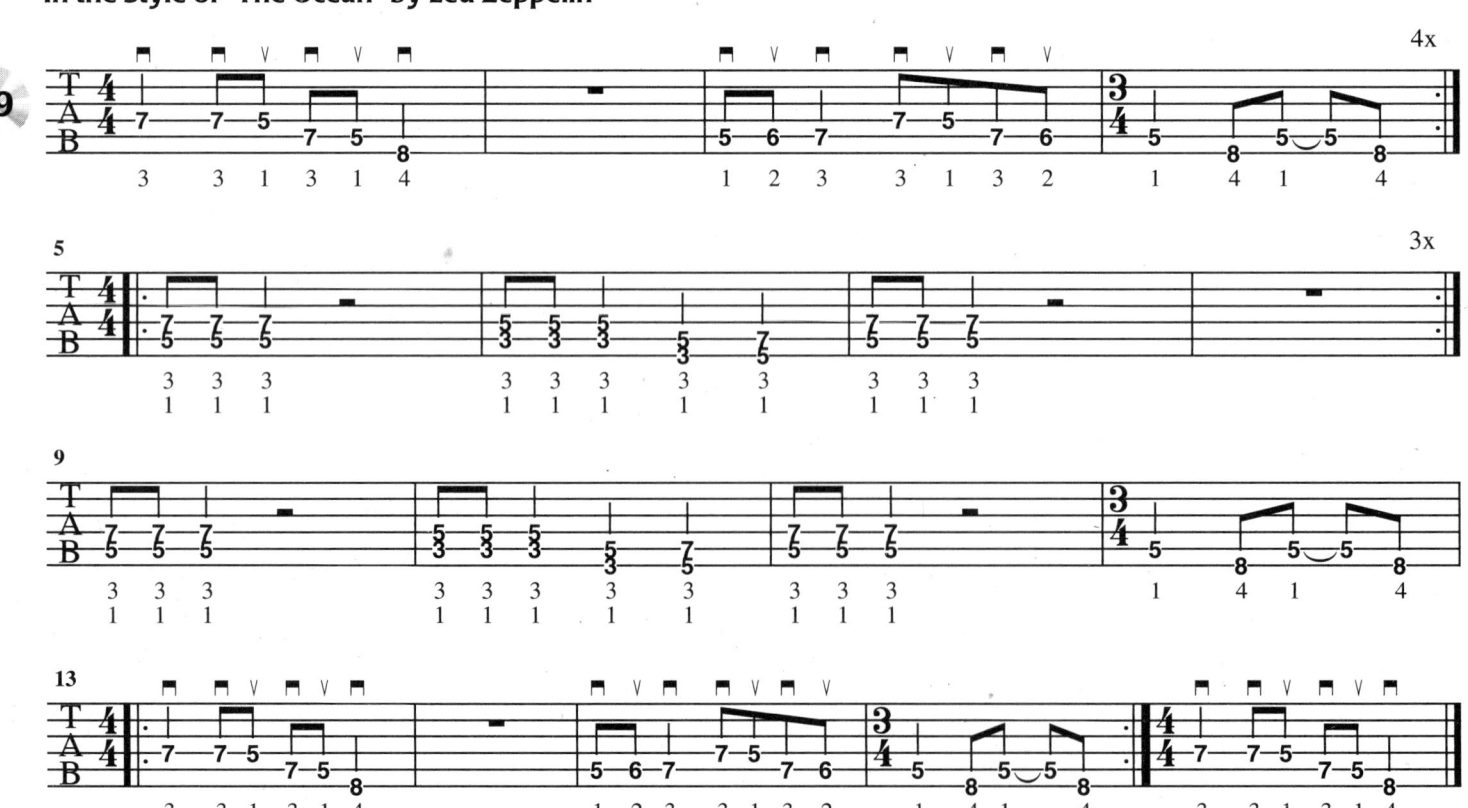

It is imperative that all beginning electric guitarists delve into the mysteries of "Iron Man" by Black Sabbath. Don't be afraid to menacingly pronounce the words "I am Iron Man" into the nearest fan, then crank up your amp and belt out this Sabbath anthem. Watch out for the dotted notes in measures 3 and 19.

In the Style of "Iron Man" by Black Sabbath

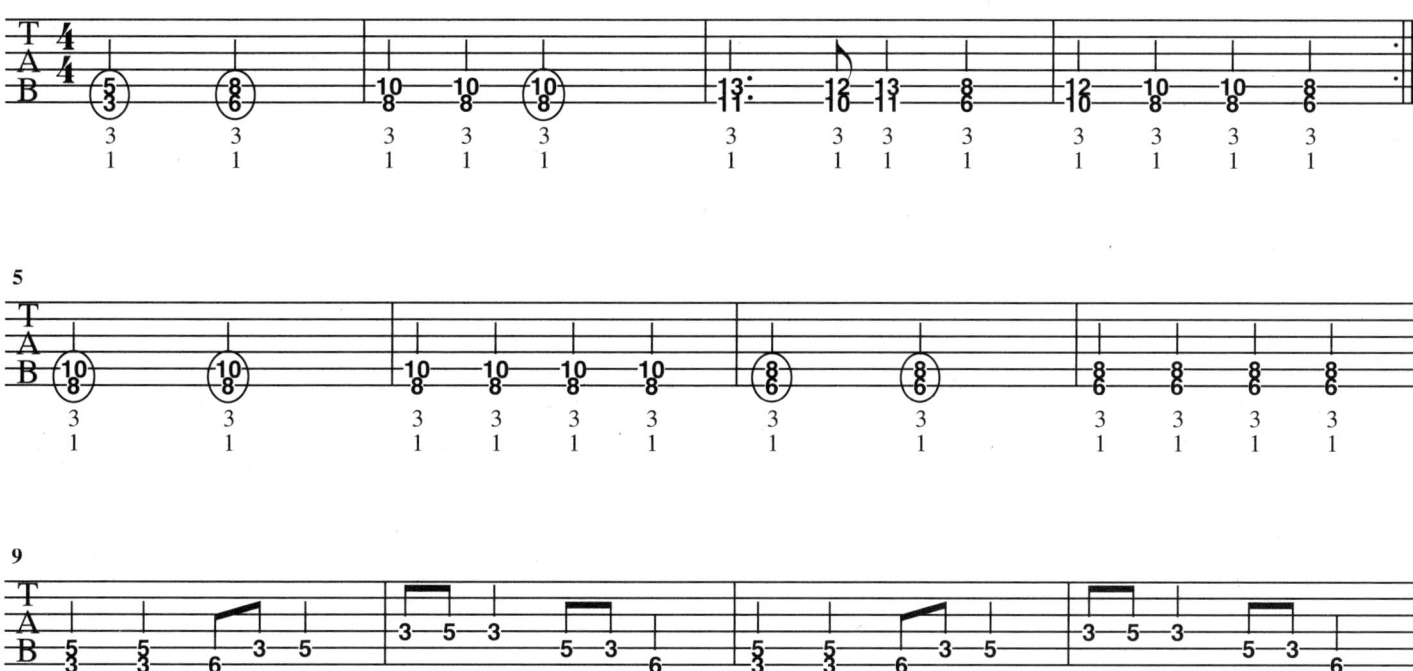

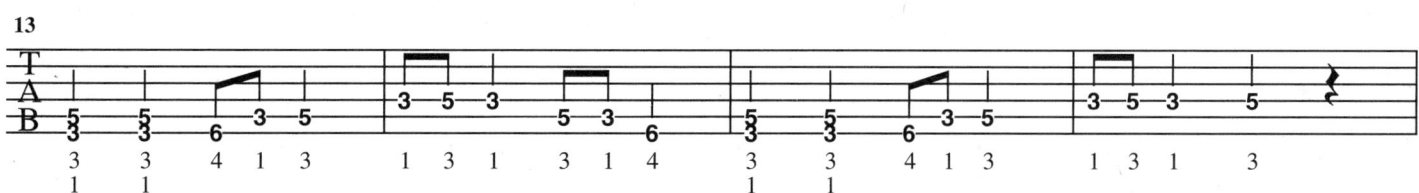

LESSON 12: DROP-D TUNING

Drop-D tuning is a beginning guitarist's dream. Not only does it make it really easy to play power chords, but by dropping the low-E string a *whole step* (the distance of two frets) to D, you get a lower, darker, and heavier sound—and who doesn't love that?

So, go ahead and lower your 6th string to D. You can do this by matching it to the open 4th string. Although this note is an octave higher, you can still tell when the 6th string reaches the D—the vibrations created by out-of-tune strings will stop. Listen to Track 71 to hear how this sounds.

Now, play the bottom three strings open, and behold...

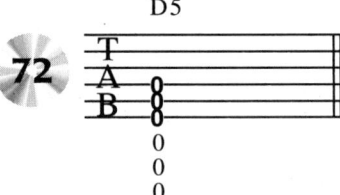

Barring

We need to learn one more technique, and it's called *barring*. To *barre* (indicated in chord diagrams with the symbol ⎯) is to press, or lay, a single finger across two or more adjacent strings at the same fret. An example of this would be to lay your 1st finger across the 4th, 5th, and 6th strings at the 3rd fret. This gives you an F5 chord. (Remember, the 6th string was lowered a whole step, so the note on the 3rd fret of the 6th string is now F instead of G.)

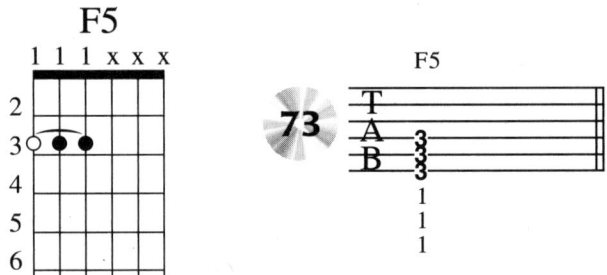

Now, try moving the chord around to the 5th fret, 8th fret, 2nd fret, etc. Wherever you place it, you get a great sounding power chord. Place it at the 5th fret and you get G5; place it at the 10th fret and you get C5, etc.

You can use any left-hand finger to barre. Check out the following exercise, and observe how heavy you've become.

Drop D Exercise

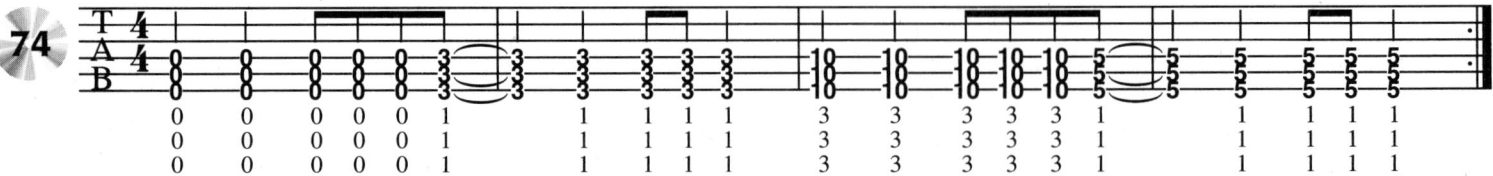

Now, try moving this chord form around the neck to create your own riffs.

Following is a song in the style of the "Father of Grunge," Neil Young. It is a drop-D classic. Watch the picking indications and dotted eighth notes in measures 5–8 and 13–16. Remember (page 36), a dot adds one half of a note's value to itself. An eighth note is half of a beat, a dot adds a quarter of a beat, so a dotted eighth note equals three quarters of a beat (1-e-&, or an eighth note tied to a sixteenth note). Your fingers will be jumping around the fretboard quite a bit on this one, so it may take some practice.

In the Style of "Cinnamon Girl" by Neil Young

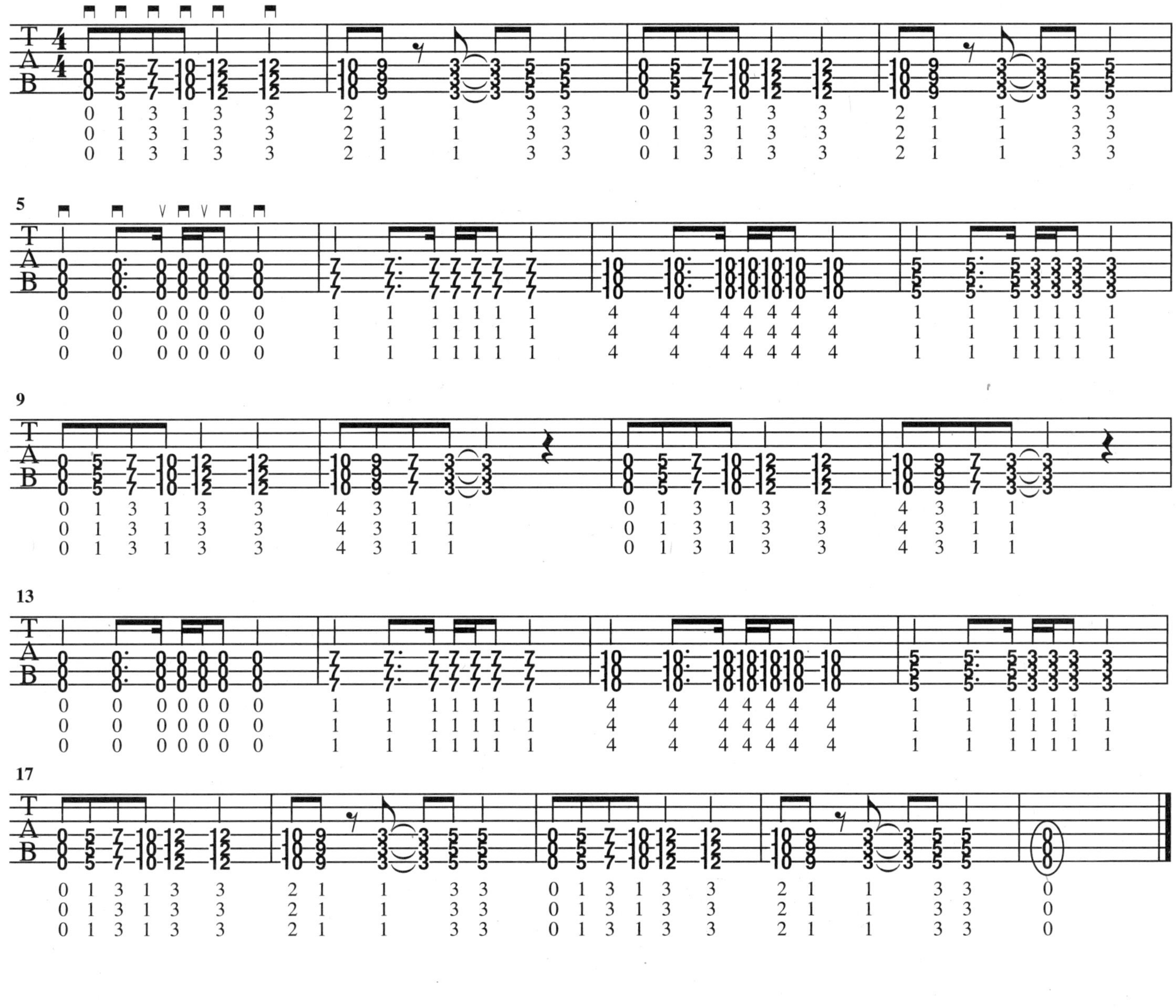

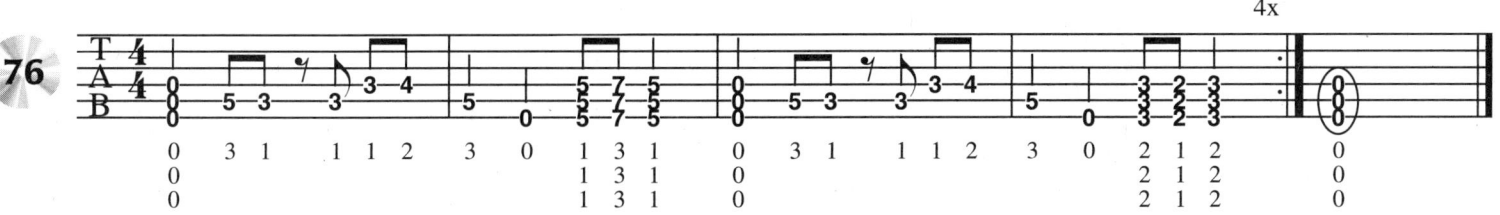

We'll end with a riff in the style of a song that makes great use of drop-D tuning. You will be using open power chords, moveable power chords, and single-note riffs on multiple strings.

In the Style of "Killing in the Name Of" by Rage Against the Machine

CONCLUSION

Congratulations! You made it to the end of *The Beginner's Guide to Electric Guitar.* But, guess what...yep, your electric journey is just beginning. Now, it's time to let go of my hand and be free, little rock bird. Jump from the nest and test your fledgling wings. Don't be afraid! You now possess many of the tools needed to really start your studies on the electric guitar.

At this point, if you don't already have one, you may consider finding a good teacher. There really is no substitute for the guidance that a good teacher can offer. In the long run, this will save you a lot of time, too; a teacher can correct your mistakes on the spot, stop you from developing bad habits, give you pointers, and show you valuable shortcuts.

There are also several books you can get to further your studies, either with a teacher or without:

- *Beginning Rock Guitar*—Paul Howard (14199) Book & CD
- *Beginning Blues Guitar*—David Hamburger (8230) Book & CD
- *Beginning Jazz Guitar*—Jody Fisher (14120) Book & CD
- *The Total Rock Guitarist*—Tobias Hurwitz (24423) Book & CD
- *The Total Blues Guitarist*—Dennis McCumber (24420) Book & CD
- *The Total Jazz Guitarist*—Jody Fisher (24417) Book & CD
- *Beginning Blues & Rock Theory for Guitar*—(21962) Book & CD
- *Guitar Shop: Getting Your Sound*—Tobias Hurwitz (18424) Book & CD
- *Teach Yourself Guitar Repair & Maintenance*—John Carruthers (22856) Book & DVD

Most importantly, play as much as you can. If you love music, listen to music all the time, love the guitar, and play the guitar all the time, there is no question that you will become a good guitar player. For your listening pleasure, below is a list of great electric guitarists and classic recordings. Good luck, and remember to stop practicing *just before* your fingers start to bleed (a joke, of course).

Listening Guide

Rock Guitarists

Jimi Hendrix—*Axis: Bold as Love; Are You Experienced*

Eddie Van Halen—*Van Halen*

Jimmy Page (Led Zeppelin)—*Led Zeppelin II; Led Zeppelin IV*

Tony Iommi (Black Sabbath)—*Paranoid; Black Sabbath; Vol. 4*

Angus Young (AC/DC)—*Highway to Hell; Back in Black*

Kirk Hammett (Metallica)—*Master of Puppets; ...And Justice for All*

Blues Guitarists

Stevie Ray Vaughan—*Couldn't Stand the Weather; Texas Flood*

B. B. King—*Live at the Regal; Completely Well; Live in Cook County Jail*

Albert King—*Born Under a Bad Sign; Live Wire/Blues Power*

Buddy Guy—*Stone Crazy; Buddy Guy & Junior Wells Play the Blues*

Jazz Guitarists

Grant Green—*Idle Moments; Grant's First Stand; Standards*

Wes Montgomery—*Smokin' at the Half Note; The Incredible Jazz Guitar of Wes Montgomery*

Pat Martino—*El Hombre; Footprints*

APPENDIX: GUITAR FRETBOARD CHART

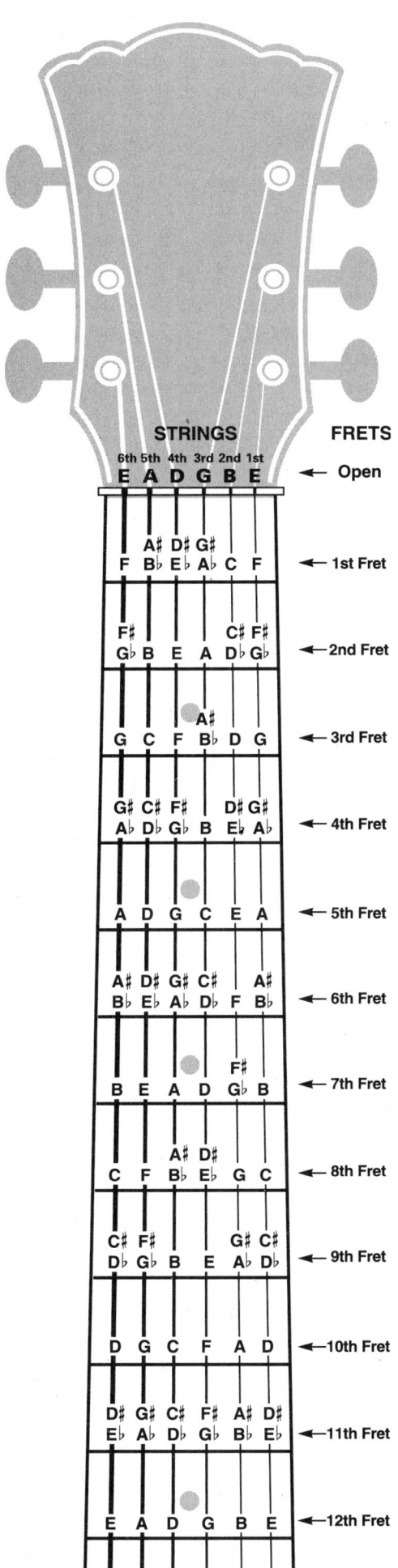

To the left is an illustration of a guitar fretboard. It shows you the names of all the notes on frets 1–12 of every string (the note names simply start over at the 12th fret). For example, if you go to the 5th fret of the 6th string, you'll see that the note is A. If you go to the 7th fret of the 5th string, you'll see that the note is E, etc.

Some frets have two names. For example, if you go to the 1st fret of the 4th string, you'll see the note names D♯ (D-sharp) and E♭ (E-flat).* These are called *enharmonic equivalents.* Enharmonic equivalents sound exactly the same and are played in the same exact location. However, they can be referred to by either name, depending on the musical situation.

Use this chart to help you memorize the notes on the bottom two strings (at least), as these are where your chord roots are commonly located.

* A *sharp* (♯) raises the pitch of a note by one fret.
 A *flat* (♭) lowers the pitch of a note by one fret.